BEING DIFFERENT MATTERS

by Wendeline de Zan and Forrest Wright

Copyright © 2017 Wendeline de Zan and Forrest Wright

Published by Page 90 Publishing

Interior Graphics/Art Credit: Chelsea Flaming

Author services by Pedernales Publishing, LLC
www. pedernalespublishing.com

Because of the dynamic nature of the Internet, any web addresses or links contained in this book may have changed since publication and may no longer be valid.

ISBN: 978-0-9996375-0-0 Paperback edition
ISBN: 978-0-9996375-1-7 Digital edition

Library of Congress Control Number: 2017917804

Printed in the United States of America

You will land your next job or client not by telling them what you have done in the past

but by convincing them of the value you will deliver in the future.

This book shows you how to do just that.

"Ditch your ideas on what a résumé should be and apply this introspective approach on how to tell your story in a persuasive and captivating way." — Hanna Hanna, Talent Acquisition Leader

"I found your book an excellent resource, in particular, the 'benefi t mill' and the 'so what' technique... very very helpful!" — Haya Morganstern, founder of Kwalified

"Going step by step through this workbook completely changed the way I view myself as an asset to an organization." — Michael Craig, successful jobseeker and first edition customer

Being Different Matters

SECOND EDITION

The Jobseeker's Manual To the New Economy

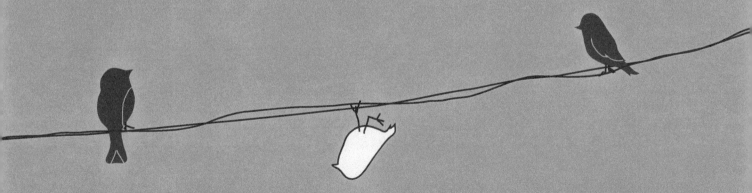

WENDELINE DE ZAN & FORREST WRIGHT   *Illustrated by Chelsea Flaming*

ICON KEY

 DO THIS

 JOT IT DOWN

 PAUSE HERE

 TAKE A CLOSER LOOK

CO-AUTHORS

Being Different Matters was written by leadership educator and executive coach, Wendeline de Zan and Forrest Wright, founder of branding agency Page 90. Wendeline helps individuals, teams, and organizations to transform their mindsets, enhance their interpersonal skills, and evolve their behaviors. Forrest, a film producer turned marketing consultant, focuses on maximizing the potential of corporations, groups and individuals through the creation of clearly differentiated brand stories.

WENDELINE DE ZAN

FORREST WRIGHT

TABLE OF CONTENTS

a story

the traditional résumé doesn't work anymore

15   IS THIS BOOK FOR YOU?

16   HOW THIS BOOK WORKS

ch. 1 / burn your résumé

20   *exercise 1*   REALITY CHECK

25   *exercise 2*   BURN YOUR RÉSUMÉ

ch. 2 / think like the boss

31   *exercise 3*   SWOT

38   *exercise 4*   TALK TO YOUR CUSTOMER

43   *exercise 5*   PAVES (YOU)

ch. 3 / focus on your benefits

52   *exercise 6*   PAVES (THE JOB)

60   *exercise 7*   THE BENEFIT MILL

67   *exercise 8*   SET YOURSELF APART

73   *exercise 9*   CONNECT THE DOTS

ch. 4 / find the right match

76   *exercise 10*   REBUILDING YOUR RÉSUMÉ

87   *exercise 11*   THE MATCH GAME

ch. 5 / speak the truth

102   *exercise 12*   SWEAR YOUR WAY TO THE TOP

appendix

110   SAMPLE RÉSUMÉS

119   SAMPLE P.A.V.E.S. AND COVER LETTERS

126   NOW WHAT?

129   THANK YOUS

A STORY

Years ago, I worked with an MBA student whose story impacted my thinking profoundly. His name is Raj, and he changed his future by rewriting his past.

Before I met Raj, he had an engineering degree. He worked for Schlumberger, an oil-drilling company. Raj spent months at a time in the middle of the Saudi Arabian desert, looking for places to drill for oil. After doing this for five or six years, Raj decided to make a career change, and so he went to business school for an MBA. That's where I met him, as his professor. While Raj's peers were focused almost exclusively on getting good grades, he decided to use the time to also build meaningful relationships and develop his professional "soft skills."

When the MBA coursework was over, final exams and job interviews nearly overlapped. Raj could have stressed studying above all other activities, like almost everyone else. He didn't. Instead, he and another like-minded student spent hours every day, for weeks, interviewing each other. It wasn't long, however, before they realized their stock interview answers sounded similar, generic. How would anyone tell the two of them apart from each other, let alone from the dozens of other MBA students similarly qualified and applying for the same jobs? To really stand out, Raj knew he needed to go deeper.

Raj's true differences lay not in his qualifications (after all, they would both have an MBA) but in the results of his work. Through dialogue and practice, Raj learned to talk not just about what he is and what he does, but what he could do for a potential employer. Intuitively, he understood that if you want someone else to see your point, it works best to take on their perspective.

When Raj interviewed with a Swiss pharmaceutical company for the most coveted job offer on campus, he thought, "What could possibly link my past engineering work with Schlumberger, an oil driller, to that of a pharmaceutical company? Why would they want me?"

It wasn't a rhetorical question: he really wondered how the company would benefit from having him on board. Out of this thought process arose a winning idea. Raj told the interviewer, "Just like I helped Schlumberger find oil in the desert, I will help you find drugs that will make you money." He painted a picture that aligned the vast oil fields of Saudi Arabia with the endless sea of drug discovery. In both cases, the risks were high and the potential reward was great. It all depended on whether the right person helmed the search. Raj framed himself as that one-in-a-million person.

Imagine being the interviewer sitting in front of Raj. Here you have a candidate who tells you that he is comfortable with risk because he has experience in an equally high-risk circumstance as that for which you are now hiring. What's more, one could easily argue that Raj experienced even greater uncertainty than someone in pharmaceuticals would ever face, given that more information exists on drugs and the market for them than on where to dig for oil.

Not surprisingly, Raj and his interviewing friend were the only two graduates to which the Swiss pharmaceutical offered jobs. Raj has been working there ever since, helping them dig for profit.

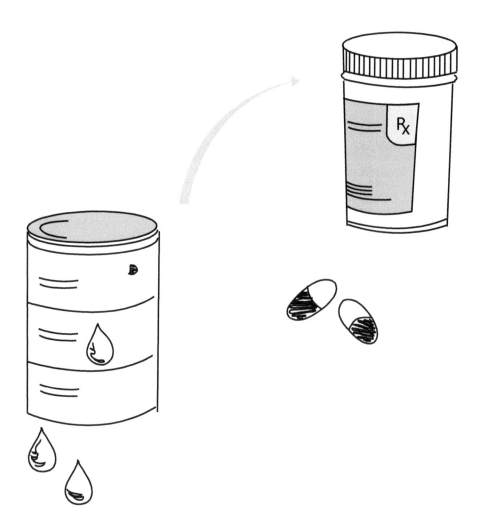

After reading Raj's story, can you also see how he could help ANY company make money in just about any field? He translated his experience from one field to another by describing his past with the perspective of his future employer's benefit. He made his résumé relevant and relatable. That will be your task while reading this book: connecting the stories of your past to your vision of the future.

"

YOU MUST STUDY THE PAST IF YOU WOULD DEFINE THE FUTURE.

– CONFUCIUS

THE TRADITIONAL RÉSUMÉ
DOESN'T WORK ANYMORE

My Uncle Dave worked at Xerox in the 1960s, when Xerox was the Apple of their time. I imagine those early days like an episode of Mad Men, as he and his colleagues built a technology empire between martini lunches and Atlantic City conventions. Uncle Dave wore a tie and jacket every day, commuting to Baltimore Monday through Friday. He got two weeks off each year for vacation, and I'm pretty sure he spent much of that free time doing things around the house he hadn't gotten to on his weekends, like canning tomatoes. Throughout the decades, he worked his way up the corporate ladder, exchanging one title for another, adding incremental responsibilities with incremental increases in pay. He did this for forty years. His résumé, if he ever needed one, probably looked like this:

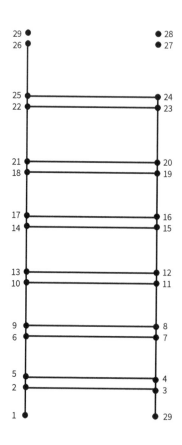

In today's new economy, this is not career reality. Upward mobility is no longer guaranteed, nor is it necessarily desired. The new career trajectory looks more like this:

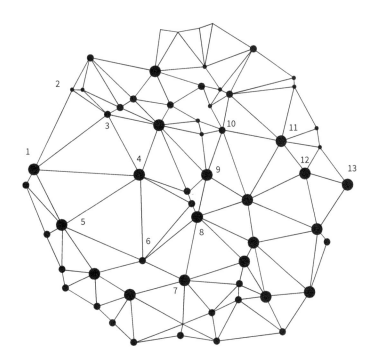

Today, someone might get a job, make a lateral move in the company, then switch companies taking a lower-paying job with better growth opportunities, go back to school or start a family, then switch careers or industries altogether and make giant leaps ahead with new clients when they strike out as independent consultants.

Sound familiar? It should. Much of today's workforce is not upwardly mobile in the traditional sense. They're just mobile.

Like our friends Josh, Mitch, Selchuk, and Carrie. In this book, you'll see how they approached their job search. They, too, have had nonlinear, nontraditional career paths.

"Your life is not a linear trajectory. There will be winds and curves and detours. Make sure to look up because, if you don't, you will miss some of those forks in the road; and it is in those opportunities that life is most interesting. And, if that opportunity scares you, that's a sign that you have to do it!"

- LISA SPINALI
1990 MBA,
freelance consultant

In fact, research shows that almost no one follows a singular career trajectory anymore. The median job tenure for a U.S. worker is 4.6 years. The average number of jobs a U.S. worker will have in a lifetime is 10.7 for women and 11.4 for men.[01]

If the majority of us are following nontraditional career paths, why are we still searching for jobs using traditional tools: the standard résumé, cover letter and same old interview prep? Part of the answer is that hiring managers require them. Why? Because people want to know that you can do what they need done, and they want to know that they can trust you to do it. They are seeking assurance. After all, their job is on the line if they don't hire the right person. Your résumé, cover letter and interview are simply tools for communicating how you are the right person for the job.

It's your job to hack the job search.

That's what this book will help you do: make traditional career tools work for nontraditional career paths so you can land the job, gig, or client you really, really want. This book will also facilitate translating those traditional career tools into modern career tools. We will do this by helping you tell your career story in a way that connects the dots between where you've been, where you are and where you want to go. Finally, this book will give you a different framework for considering what you've done and what you can do. It will teach you to differentiate yourself from others by taking the employer's perspective.

01 Bureau of Labor Statistics. (2014, September 18). Employee Tenure Summary. Retrieved July 20, 2016, from http://www.bls.gov/news.release/tenure.nr0.htm

"

CAREERS ARE MORE LIKE JUNGLE GYMS THAN LADDERS- SOMETIMES A SIDEWAYS OR BACKWARD STEP CAN PROPEL YOU FORWARD.

– SARAH ROBB O'HAGAN

president of Equinox

IS THIS BOOK FOR YOU?

This book is written for everyone out there who does not have a typical, straightforward career path. And that is just about everyone these days. Do any of these situations sound familiar?

- *Are you a freelancer who is having trouble connecting the dots of all the different projects on which you've worked?*

- *Have you made a career change (or more than one) and aren't quite sure how to explain it in the context of the new job you're pursuing?*

- *Are you applying to graduate school or about to graduate from school?*

- *Are you going into business for yourself and unsure of how best to position yourself to land clients?*

- *Have you taken time off to travel the world, pursue a dream, take care of a loved one or another life event that creates a big, fat hole in your résumé?*

- *Were you laid off and are looking for a new job?*

- *Do you want a promotion but may not be the obvious choice for the job?*

- *Did you serve in the military and are you now searching for a way to translate those skills into the workforce?*

- *Did you take time off to start a family and are now returning to the job market?*

- *Do you feel underutilized in your current role at work?*

If you can relate to any of these scenarios, this book is for you.

A word of caution: this book was written for people who not only seek a new job, project or client, but who also seek the right job, project or clients for themselves.

HOW THIS BOOK WORKS

Readers should be curious about two things: what makes them uniquely valuable, and how they can apply that value to help others. Readers should also be proactive. This book is skinny on prose and fat on exercises. This intro is the last time you'll read big blocks of text. (phew)

In here, we're going to consider the mindsets, skills, and behaviors that make you uniquely valuable. The chapters are arranged so that you will assess where you've been, where you are, and where you want to go. You will find 12 exercises.

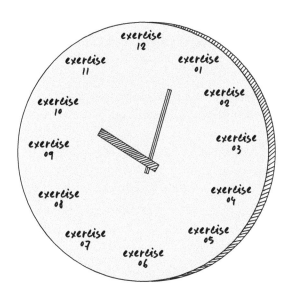

These exercises in this order is best way we know how to help you differentiate yourself in the job market while connecting the dots of your work history. If you don't connect the dots for potential employers or clients, they may make assumptions about you or your work that aren't in your favor. We don't want that to happen. We want to make it as simple as possible for you to align your unique value to their unmet, or even undiscovered, needs. These exercises are tools you can adapt time and time again as you pursue new opportunities – whatever those may be.

Complete the exercises and you'll have the following:

1.   *A revamped résumé that tells your career story and makes better sense to a potential employer*

2.   *New and improved feature/benefit statements (those are the bullet points on your résumé) that prove why you're the person the employer ought to hire.*

3.   *The ability to think like an employer*

4.   *A refreshed perspective on why you are the best candidate for the job you seek*

5.   *An understanding of what makes you uniquely valuable in a competitive job market*

6.   *A strategy for your career planning, driven by an understanding of how your past can help you get you to where you want to go*

7.   *A story that tells a potential employer or contact, succinctly and compellingly, who you are and what you do*

8.   *The ability to answer one of the toughest interview questions out there: "Tell me about yourself."*

If you're looking for quick and dirty tips on résumés, cover letters or interviews, we cover that too.

More than anything, though, we hope that in using this book you will see yourself and your future differently. It's that insight that will allow you to land the job or client you seek.

LET'S GO HACK YOUR JOB SEARCH.

chapter 1

Burn your résumé

"Only after disaster can we be resurrected."

- CHUCK PALAHNIUK, FIGHT CLUB

Like most worthwhile things, before we help you build an awesome, job-getting résumé or successful career strategy, we're going to have to test your foundation. And that might mean tearing down some of the things that aren't working, destroying preconceived notions, or wrecking what was structurally flawed in the first place. In other words, this first step might hurt a little. But it's a necessary step.

 ## REALITY CHECK

Imagine you have just met with a prospective employer or client. As you walk away from their office, consider what you want them to remember about you and complete the sentences below.

A prospective client/employer should remember:

I am...

I am...

I am...

I am...

With me, your business will...

Please do this now, and only after you do so, continue reading.

Look at your list. Now ask yourself if your competition (other job applicants) can or will claim that they are, can do, or offer the first thing on your list. If your competition would at least say that they are or can do that same thing or possess that same attribute, it does not differentiate you. Cross it out. Go down your list. Do any qualities by which you wish to be remembered remain?

All around the world, we've asked professionals this question. Their answers looked like this:

1 I am a team player.
2 I am trustworthy.
3 I am reliable.
4 I have great interpersonal and communication skills.
5 I am a hard-working self-starter.
6 I am pleasant to work with.
7 With me, your business will grow.

When we finished, their list looked like this:

1 ~~I am a team player.~~
2 ~~I am trustworthy.~~
3 ~~I am reliable.~~
4 ~~I have great interpersonal and communication skills.~~
5 ~~I am a hard-working self-starter.~~
6 ~~I am pleasant to work with.~~
7 ~~With me, your business will grow.~~

IF WHAT YOU'RE
SAYING ABOUT
YOURSELF
DOESN'T
ACTUALLY GET
YOU APART, HOW
WILL YOU BE
REMEMBERED?

You've now forced a potential employer or client to choose you (or not) based on something that doesn't distinguish you or, worse, for something other than that for which you want to be remembered. You were so focused on proving how good you were that you never articulated anything exceptional about yourself. In this day and age, "good" is not good enough.

Every job candidate IS the same, because they APPEAR the same– until they actually differentiate themselves. In the new economy, you are no different, nor better, nor more value-adding, nor more worth-spending-time-with until people understand your value.

Consider how you choose which product to buy when all the products seem the same.

Question   *What do you call an abundant supply of an undifferentiated product?*
Answer   *A commodity. (Think: Rice, Corn, and Beans)*

Question   *How do people choose among commodities?*
Answer   *Price or brand.*

Unless your strategy is to beat your competition by lowering your salary (price) or you come into a job opportunity with name recognition (brand), you must differentiate yourself based on something else. If the "something else" you are thinking of can be acquired easily (including another degree or certification), then consider that a commodity, too.

Now look at your résumé and mentally compare it to others'. Everyone else has "education," "experience" and "interests," right? So, what's so special about your education, experience and interests?

With off-shoring of service-sector jobs, and "on-shoring" of international talent, as well as a volatile global economy, more people are competing for fewer jobs. As Thomas Friedman pointed out, "The world is flat." And in a flat world, dozens, hundreds or may even thousands of other people whose qualifications match or exceed your own want the same position you want.

So, what are you going to do about it?

Let's start by your getting honest with yourself.

BURN YOUR RÉSUMÉ

Grab your résumé and a pencil.

We're going to view it with the same scrutiny as the first exercise. Take a good look at that résumé and cross off anything that is undifferentiating. Challenge yourself. Put a big red line through anything that is not exceptional. You have an MBA? Do other applicants for this job also have one? Cross it off. You can program in Python? Will the other applicants be able to do so? It gets a line through it.

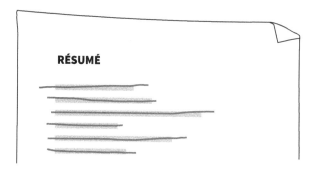

What's left? Not much? That's okay. We're not scrapping these professional accomplishments. We're showing that if you want to stand out, you need to show them more.

Look at the words and phrases remaining in your résumé. Anything jump out? Powerful words? Repeating themes? In later exercises, we'll help you take those same bullets and craft them as more exceptional entries that emphasize your differentiators and your strengths. Don't worry if you've crossed off everything on your current résumé. We'll also help you jog your memory about other accomplishments that might better sell your abilities and skills to a potential employer or client.

But for now, look at the wreckage that was your résumé.
Yikes!
Let's start fresh.

Think like the boss

"Revenue is vanity. Profit is sanity. Cash is reality."

- GREG SAVAGE

Since we are going to completely reimagine the résumé, let's start at the top. We've all seen résumés capped with a big, fat summary / objective that goes something like this:

RÉSUMÉ

Looking for a challenging, creative opportunity where I can apply my skills in a dynamic organization with plenty of room for advancement.

What an employer reads is, "Help me advance my career." Why should it be the employer's job to find a position that suits you? You are the one offering your skills. Instead of considering your employer or client as someone who takes care of you, think about how you can take care of them (i.e., add value to the company).

Better but still bad:

RÉSUMÉ

To apply the knowledge acquired through a bachelor's degree in Marketing and Communications and two summer internships at a public relations agency to an entry-level position on the marketing or PR team of a major financial institution.

This sounds like a grocery list of credentials while offering no clue as to how this person can contribute meaningfully to the organization. Why would the employer care that you've had not one, but two, summer internships? How does that qualify you for anything? Your internship may have just been making coffee and working the mailroom. (Now, if you had become the best coffee barista in the tri-city area and had increased revenues by 12% or you had completely reorganized the workflow of the mailroom to increase efficiencies by 33%, that would matter.)

Instead of listing all the reasons you think you're great, cut to the chase and tell them what they need to hear. Try to complete the following sentence. (It's a tough one)

Life will be better once you hire me because...

It's time for a mindset change from "Accommodate me" and "Look at how great I am" to "This is how I can help you" and "This is how you'll benefit from having me onboard."

When taking a stab at the dreaded "objective statement" of his résumé, our friend Josh hit the right balance between demonstrating his value and revealing his personality.

RÉSUMÉ OF JOSH

Technology evangelist with a passion for evolving products and processes beyond the obvious.

This type of summary statement worked for him as he applied for a position in marketing. Words like "evangelist," "passion" and "beyond the obvious" whet the appetite to find out more and see if his credentials really back this up. Would it work for jobs where creativity is not a virtue? Maybe. Maybe not. But it does a great job of giving the reader an insightful glimpse into who this Josh character is. And it's likely his competition wouldn't describe themselves similarly.

Our friend Mitch also blended his skills with value to a prospective employer, an academic research institute.

RÉSUMÉ OF MITCH

A social scientist at heart, my curiosity for understanding cultural phenomena and systematic irrationalities drives my research and passion in a variety of fields.

Both of these guys got the jobs they were after.

In both objective statements, the reader gets a feeling for the applicant which conveys (above all) competence in the areas of employer need and a positive sense of the applicant's personality. Yes, we said "personality." Personality matters a lot. (See sidebar on Cultural Fit.)

It's important to note that not all résumés need, or even benefit from having, a summary statement. Some people like using them; some don't. However, crafting your summary statement is a useful exercise. Kept in your proverbial back pocket, a summary statement can serve as an elevator pitch when someone asks "So, what do you do?" or "Tell me about yourself." Complete the rest of the exercises in this book, and you should be able to craft a snappy self-summary in no time.

CULTURAL FIT.

Speaking of letting your personality shine, let's talk about how your personality will jibe with a corporate culture or client. When you are researching potential companies or clients, put understanding the culture of the company at the top of your list. Why? Because it's imperative you understand if and how you might fit. Here's what business visionary Richard Branson has to say on the subject:

"The first thing to look for when searching for a great employee is somebody with a personality that fits with your company culture. Most skills can be learned, but it is difficult to train people on their personality. If you can find people who are fun, friendly, caring and love helping others, you are on to a winner."

We've talked with headhunters and HR managers at some of the world's largest companies,

(continued on page 33)

exercise 03
SWOTING YOUR TARGET

A summary statement is all about showcasing how you can help a potential client or employer. Whether you will write one or not, though, you will need a firm understanding about that employer, about yourself, and the meaningful connection between the two of you.

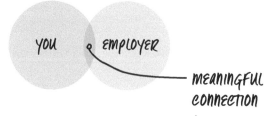

Let's start with a potential client or employer you'd really like to impress **What do you know about them and their needs?**

From your potential employer's point of view, answer the following questions:

- *What do they do?*
- *What are they good at?*
- *Where are they weak?*
- *What's happening in their part of the market/industry right now?*
- *What's on their short-term horizon? Medium-term? Long-term?*
- *Do you see any opportunities for growth/investment/money-making?*
- *Who are their competitors?*
- *Who is winning right now, and by how much?*
- *What are the goals of your Client/Employer?*
- *What's going to stop them from getting there?*
- *How can you help?*

The easiest way to get at these questions is to **SWOT** your target company.

If you're not already familiar with it, SWOT [02] is a tool that provides a quick strategic overview. When applied to a company, it has many purposes. The way we'll use it here is to get a deep enough understanding of your potential employer such that you could put yourself in their shoes and feel their pain points and successes, as well as glean insights about their future that they might or might not have considered.

At the end of the day, the only way you can add value (as opposed to drain it) is for you to know how they make money and how they can make more. To this end, consider:

S

What are they good at?
Where and how do they outcompete their competitors?

W

Where are they weak?
In what sectors are their rivals beating them?
What's going to stop them from achieving their goals?

O

What's happening in their part of the market/industry right now?
What's on their short-term horizon? Medium term? Long term?
Do you see any opportunities for growth/investment/money-making?

T

Who else does the same? List the top 2-3 competitors.
Who is winning right now, and by how much?
What was the last year like for them?
What are the market conditions now?
What are analysts saying is not going well?

02   SWOT is an acronym for Strengths, Weaknesses, Opportunities and Threats and is a framework commonly used in business.

and Susan F. of a fortune 500 company with over 115,000 employees worldwide captured an overwhelming sentiment when she said this:

"When choosing a company to work for, candidates often focus on benefits, pay, industry and other obvious attributes. However, to find true corporate nirvana, a candidate should focus on how their core values and personality blend with the corporate culture of their prospective employer."

An effective way to keep perspective is to begin the interview process with clearly defined expectations on both sides of the table. This includes asking questions regarding the big picture view of the role and the details of the everyday grind.

Do not assume that if you are right for the role that you are right for the company.

Interviewing for a job is no different from any other long-term relationship.

Take Google (aka Alphabet) as an example. [03] To go deeper, research their background as well.

STRENGTHS

- Open source products and services
- Quality and customer experience are the primary objects
- Financial situation
- Access to the widest group of internet users worldwide
- Strong patents portfolio
- Product Integration
- Culture of innovation

WEAKNESSES

- Relies on one source of income
- Unprofitable products
- Patent litigations
- Consumer fears about privacy

OPPORTUNITIES

- Growing number of mobile Internet users
- Obtaining patents through acquisitions
- Driverless electronic cars
- Growing into electronics industry and wearables
- Google fiber cables

THREATS

- Growing number of mobile Internet users
- Unprofitable products
- EU antitrust laws
- Competition from Microsoft
- Privacy-fueled lawsuits

To answer these questions without the benefit of an inside connection to the employer, begin with a Google search with keywords "SWOT" and your company name, or go to a site like Indeed, SimplyHired, LinkedIn, or a paid service like OneSource or try

03   Downloaded on 23 February 2016 from
http://www.marketing91.com/google-swot-analysis/

Bloomberg.com + the company's name and check out their company profiles. You should be able to produce a decent overview. Also check out the employer or client's website, especially the "About Us" section. This will give you insight into how they perceive themselves (at least, how they officially position themselves). What you are looking for is what THEY (the employers) think the answers to these questions are.

COMPANY BACKGROUND

Name	Google, Inc
Industries served	Internet (Google Search, Google AdWords, Gmail) Computer software (Chrome OS, Picasa, Google Earth) Consumer electronics (Chromebook, Nexus, Google TV)
Geographic areas served	Worldwide (more than 50 countries)
Headquarters	Mountain View, California, U.S.
Current CEO	Sundar Pichai.
Revenue	US$66.001 billion (2014) 18.8% increase over US$55.519 billion (2013)
Profit	US$14.444 billion (2014) 11.8% increase over US$12.920 billion
Employees	53,600 (2015)
Parent	Alphabet Inc.
Main Competitors	Apple Inc., Facebook Inc., Microsoft Corporation, Samsung Electronics Co., Ltd., International Business Machines Corporation and many other Internet, computer software and consumer electronics companies.

Get to know the company as much as possible before you commit to them, and they commit to you."

It's also useful to research if and how the corporation fosters community: events, charitable causes, social mixers, leagues, etc. Can you demonstrate an overlap in interests between you and the corporate community outside of the actual work you do? This is where those "interests" you find at the bottom of a résumé could actually be germane.

While researching community, why not jump on to LinkedIn to see if there is some common ground between you and the interviewers so you can build the conversation on a personal level? [04]

Take time to do this now for a dream employer/client. Yes, we said dream employer/client." Come on, we know there's at least one company you'd like to work for or some client you'd like to land.

Now that you've done exercise 3, can you see how SWOTing a company provides you the intel to better position yourself? You're not finished yet, though! The next step is to synthesize (not summarize) what all the information means for you and your job search. Your synthesis doesn't need to be brilliant: it just needs to be relevant and meaningful. For example, our generalized synthesis of Google tells us that despite becoming a more mature company they are highly competitive, always looking for the best talent, and the likelihood that they will continue

04   "5 Interview Skills That Will Get You Hired," by Nicole Fallon, Business News Daily Contributor, downloaded on 24 November 2017 from (http://news.yahoo.com/5-interview-skills-hired-121155266.html)

WHEN A COMPANY IS BIG ENOUGH, AT ANY GIVEN POINT, THEY NEED NEW BLOOD TO REPLACE SOMEONE WHO'S BEEN PROMOTED, REPOSITIONED, OR HAS LEFT.

CARRIE EXPLORES
THE AD COUNCIL
(An Example of SWOT Synthesis)

What do they do?
Remind the public of the things they should already be doing.

What are they good at?
Stopping and attracting attention to critical matters.

Where are they weak?
In moving folks from awareness to action (hard to change behavior without having a funded incentive or regulatory effect).

What's happening in their part of the market/industry right now?
There's lots of other nonprofits utilizing the same channels - all pushing for their outcomes, funding their campaign, the Ad Council is one voice among many in the fight for good.

(continued on page 39)

hiring is medium to high. Even when they are tightening their belt. When a company is big enough, at any given point, they need new blood to replace someone who's been promoted, repositioned, or has left.

Given the SWOT above (and given that we know people who work there), we believe it would be worth applying to Google if you graduated with a degree in engineering and/or have written an amazing piece of software, are driven by excellence rather than rules, and prefer a casual work environment to a formal one. These basic insights could be the starting point for your job search strategy.

Imagine that you've completed your SWOT for your dream employer and have synthesized what that information means for the company. You have an educated guess as to what is in the mind of someone who works there (what worries them and what makes them proud). Is that enough to make you interesting in an interview? You have synthesized public knowledge only—stuff that is out there in the public domain. Knowing what is in their annual report communicates interest in them, but will hardly make you interesting.

Uh-oh.

exercise 04

TALK TO CUSTOMERS AND PARTNERS

To catch the attention of executives [05] in your target company, you must possess a unique perspective about that company. How do you get it?

Some very good friends of ours run an equity research firm.[06] Their analysis is usually spot-on and insightful, and it helps investment banks make predictions about the stock market. For this service, investment banks pay our friends a lot of money.

To be able to provide this service, our friends need to be more knowledgeable than anyone else. How do our friends get information that isn't readily available?

They talk to all kinds of people all along the value chain of companies they cover. To truly understand the market and where it is heading, they also talk to companies (and attend trade shows) peripherally associated with the companies they cover. They ask people what they think of their target company's next "it" product and whether it will succeed or fail and why. They then synthesize all the information and give it actionable meaning. This process gives them a unique perspective, and they do it so effectively that CEOs clamber to meet with them.

How can you be like our friends and acquire a unique perspective ?[07]

---

05   If you are interviewing with Human Resources (HR) personnel only, knowing about the company is usually enough. When interviewing with executives and others who make decisions about the company's operations, having unique knowledge differentiates you.

06   Essentially, they figure out how much a company should be worth, given its current performance and strategy. www.crossresearch.com

07   It is worth noting that having a "Unique Perspective" is quite different from having "Unique Information." When you have a perspective, it means that you took information and added value to it. When you just have information, you leave it to the listener to decide what the meaning behind it is.

What's on their short-term horizon? Medium-term? Long-term?

Short-term is bring old and new critical social issues to the limelight. Mid-term help increase everyday awareness of them and curb behaviors. Long-term- eradicate these issues (drunk driving, forest fires, texting when driving).

Do you see any opportunities for growth/investment/money-making?

Related social benefits of saved lives, reduced health/liability issues. Positive spillover benefits.

Who are their competitors?

Every nonprofit you know.

Who is winning right now, and by how much?

Define winning. If winning is saving one life, they are playing a part. Other nonprofits are more focused on one issue/cause and thus probably make greater strides in single areas. Ad Council supports cross sec-

(continued on page 41)

Find out what it is like to do business with Company X, whether that's as a customer, an employee, or a partner in their supply chain.

Good questions include the following:

- *What specifically does Company X do that delights customers?*

- *What do you wish Company X would do/what could Company X do to make your job easier?*

- *How does Company X demonstrate that you can trust them?*

- *When you do business with Company X, how do you feel?*

- *How efficient is Company X in creating value for customers?*

- *How could Company X serve you better?*

- *Who makes products a, b, and c better than Company X does?*

- *Which company provides better service than Company X and why?*

- *Why do you buy from Company X instead of Company Y?*

- *What would make you switch?*

Pick a company you'd like to work for. See if you can identify at least two or more people like the ones listed here who can help you with your research:

1   *An employee. Someone who works there, used to work there, or knows someone who worked there and can put you in touch. MBA students often set up an "informational interview." That means they drop their agenda of looking for a job and simply set up a friendly face-to-face to ask questions and gain insights on that company. It's a great way to introduce oneself and learn about a company with no pressure on the interviewer or the interviewee.*

2   *A customer. If you can't find one, go be one. Be your own secret shopper.*

3   *A partner. Someone who works for a company that does or did business with them.*

4   *A competitor. Someone who works for or owns a competitive solution. What do they see as your company's strengths and weaknesses?*

This is where social media, especially a site like LinkedIn, can really pay off as a research tool. After you find these people, reach out to them for answers to your questions.

After you get these answers from people along their value chain and from competitors, you have both outsider knowledge (SWOT) and an insider perspective regarding how others view the company you are applying for. Your ability to demonstrate industry knowledge will give you credibility and shows interest, and you will have a unique perspective that people from within the company may not have. Do you think that an executive would be interested in how others in their value chain view them? Of course s/he would. To make you even more interesting, link Company X's needs to what you can offer.

tor initiatives (so not clear game of winning or losing) but in learning from what's working in all the individual cases and using these tactics going forward.

What are the goals of your Client/Employer?

"Inspiring Change. Improving lives. Our mission is to identify a select number of significant public issues and stimulate action on those issues through communications programs that make a measurable difference in our society."

To that end, the Ad Council marshals volunteer talent from the advertising and communications industries, the facilities of the media, and the resources of the business and nonprofit communities to create awareness, foster understanding and motivate action.

What's going to stop them from getting there?

Lack of funding, growth of competing non profits, government regulation.

(continued on page 43)

their need

Their needs are what stop them from accomplishing their goals. What could you offer to help them get out of that hole? What do you want to offer?

Ah...is it sinking in yet?

your offer

You are not applying for a job.

You are applying for an opportunity to help Company X achieve its goals.

That is how you begin to think like a boss. Instead of thinking how the company can help you, think about how you can help the company.

It's time to see how you are (or are not) uniquely suited to do exactly that.
To accomplish this, it is not enough to know what you can do. We also want you to know what you have done, what you would do if only you could, and what you would not like to do even if you had to.

Why? We feel joy in the process of doing what we're good at. For a while, during childhood, we do this naturally. But somewhere along the way, we forget it, and we try to please others, or we just try to get stuff done. In all the busywork of life, getting degrees, finding a job, and starting and maintaining a family or home, we forget what we want and why we want it. We end up in jobs that don't bring us happiness but somehow help us pay our bills. If that's the case with you, is it any wonder that you're not enthusiastic about finding another unfulfilling job?

For a few moments, let's get out of that mentality and get back to knowing ourselves and identifying what gives us meaning.[08]

---

08 Money is not a motivating factor. Money doesn't thrill me or make me play better because there are benefits to being wealthy. I'm just happy with a ball at my feet. My motivation comes from playing the game I love. If I wasn't paid to be a professional footballer I would willingly play for nothing. - Lionel Messi, Barcelona FC. 4 time winner of the Ballon d'or; https://genius.com/Lionel-messi-messis-career-honours-annotated Download date 24 November 2017.

exercise 05
P.A.V.E.S (YOU)

Take a blank sheet of paper, orient it lengthwise (horizontally), and draw two vertical lines such that it's divided into three columns. Now draw a line across the middle of the page so you have six sections. Each section represents a category listed below. Write your own examples under each one of them. (We like writing this, as opposed to typing it up, because there is something organic about the process that may inspire more insights) My blank sheet looks like this:

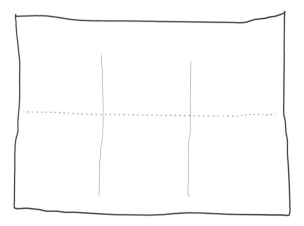

Passions.

This is the first section on your worksheet. What activities do you enjoy? It also could be (in the words of a very out-of-the-box thinker) "things that you almost never not want to do." For this and the other sections, we're looking for answers that are personal and professional. Don't limit yourself to one or the other.

- *Building engines*
- *Helping others*
- *Reading philosophy*
- *Collecting Pez dispensers*
- *Traveling*
- *Going to the theatre*
- *Getting to know new cultures*
- *Playing team sports*

Forrest's PASSIONS: Making movies, urban travel, vegetable gardening, making corporate presentations not suck, throwing themed parties, beach boot camp, the Oscars, screenwriting, backyard chickens.

Wendeline's PASSIONS: understanding what makes people tick, traveling, exercising, discovering new music, boots, Nikki, neurobiology, gardening, extraordinary experiences, philosophy, art, friends.

Accomplishments

Name and write down anything that you feel pride in having done. The act itself need not be amazing. This is about something that made YOU feel good. It does not have to be a professionally related accomplishment, either. The only rule: be specific!

- *Speaking at your brother's wedding*
- *Scoring highly on your evaluations*
- *Creating something everyone liked and appreciated*
- *Increasing sales by 20%*
- *Despite everyone's advice to the contrary, making it on your own*

Forrest's Accomplishments: producing a feature film before I turned 30, selling a $10M project to a Fortune 500 CEO, starting Shark Tank at my business school, writing a feature-length script, completing the CA AIDS Ride, riding my bike from San Francisco to LA.

Wendeline's Accomplishments: extensive international travel and living abroad, self-reliance from a young age, blending in with people from many cultures, working at the World Bank in my 20s, holding my own with very accomplished people in many fields.

Values
—

What is necessary or desirable for you in work and life?

- *Economic security*
- *Fame*
- *Freedom*
- *Knowledge*
- *Autonomy*
- *Leadership*
- *Responsibility and accountability*
- *Friendship*
- *Respect*
- *Loyalty*
- *Trust*
- *Achievement*
- *Creativity*
- *Challenge*

Forrest's values: change and newness, dreaming big and audacious goals, encouragement and feedback, time off and flexible schedule, creativity, intellectual stimulation, working with high-functioning teams.

Wendeline's values: friendships, sensuality, creativity, openness, kindness, flexibility, intellectual drive, working well with people.

Experiences.

—

Consider events that made you who you are today and that you enjoyed or took pleasure in. Again, be as specific as you can.

- *Traveling all over the world, especially Iceland*
- *Saving unprotected rainforest in Brazil*
- *Working at an international company*
- *Working with much older and much younger people than myself*
- *Managing a team of 25*
- *Winning a championship golf tournament*
- *Meditating for 10 days straight*

Forrest's experiences: white water rafting, backpacking solo through Europe, moving to California alone, traveling the world with a movie crew.

Wendeline's experiences: living abroad for years in many cities; traveling to many countries for work and pleasure and building relationships with people there; working for small and large companies; creating extraordinary experiences for people that they would never have experienced without me.

Skills.

—

What abilities have you acquired or were you born with that you'd want to use again? If you will be acquiring skills or training, put those down, too. *

- *Speaking Spanish and German*
- *An eye for spelling and grammar*
- *Web design*
- *Ability to connect with different people*
- *Excellence in public speaking*
- *Programming in Drupal*
- *Project Management*
- *Reading a P & L statement*

Forrest's skills: delivering pitches, interviewing others, empathic listening, big concept dreaming, public speaking, finding the heart of the problem, creating the big cinematic experience, motivating/inspiring change, telling someone the truth that's staring right at them but that they're not acknowledging.

Wendeline's Skills: communicating and building trust and rapport with most people and animals, leadership development, public speaking, teaching at a graduate and executive level, writing, patience and ability to handle difficult people and situations, helping others think through complex interpersonal situations, conflict resolution, sales training.

Trash Can

We added an additional category because there are certain things that we don't ever want to do again. That category is called, "Trash Can." Put your undesirables there.

- *Work alone*
- *Doing highly detailed work*
- *Reporting to someone else*
- *Traveling the majority of the time*
- *Hands-off management*
- *Be in a low- or high-stress environment*

Forrest's Trash Can: working alone all of the time, being responsible for the budget, working on the same project for more than a few months, internal creative teams with little or no turnover (i.e. stagnant), ugly workspaces with bad lighting and ugly furniture

Wendeline's Trash Can: logistical support, Excel spreadsheets, work with bland people whose lives are about pursuing nothing personal or excellent, having to work alone for long periods of time.

This is what a completed PAVES sheet looks like:

Okay. Go to your local coffee shop and jack yourself up on lattes. This isn't going to be as hard as you think if you just dive right in. Completing your PAVES is going to have a big payoff when it's time to finish your résumé.

Passions.

Meeting new people
Helping people
Traveling
Writing/Journaling
Being creative
Finding new music
Art
Theatre

Accomplishments

Taught many hundreds of strangers
Married for 11 years
Moving + Adapting so many times
Organizing many cultural events
Winning speech contests high school

Values

Freedom
Security
Friendships
Ability to do new things
Provocative conversation
Playfulness
Good food and wine
Being/looking physically fit

Experiences

Traveling at a young age to very foreign cultures
active in High School
Moving to India
Experimenting with diff people
Moving to London
Working in Haiti during 92-97
Living in Mexico City

Skills

Can Build rapport quickly
Can spot good music/groups
Can translate concepts into examples
Can persuade people
Can get people to open up
Can energize others

Trash Can

Admin stuff
Math-heavy work
Working alone for long periods
Being with only 1 type of person.

Go ahead and do it now. We'll wait.

Now that you have completed your PAVES, do you notice some common themes surfacing from it? Are there things you mention again and again? What are they? Take a moment and write them down.   If you don't keep seeing the same thing again and again, try identifying similar types of things and circling those.

~~~~~~~~~

In the example above, a common theme is people. Wendeline likes meeting them, spending time with them, and befriending them. She also likes to meet different types from different cultures around the globe. From this we can surmise a general interest and proficiency in working with diverse groups of people. She would not be well-suited for a job that sticks her in a cubicle with little social interaction.

Other themes we've spotted:

- *Adaptation: the ability to mix and meld successfully with people from all backgrounds. Lots of people like to travel and are interested in other cultures. But how many people actually thrive in different cultures? This is the chameleon quality.*
- *Rapport: this trait transcends an ability to meet others and includes actually building deeper relationships, which can be leveraged for more meaningful transactions. Rapport earns trust, and trust is the lubrication of persuasion. If you're a business, you want this person on your team.*
- *Culture: food, theater, art, etc. Employing the artistic side of life to appreciate and connect with other cultures*
- *International: this person definitely has a bit of gypsy in her and loves traveling. Matched with the other themes, we can begin to see how a multi-national corporation could really benefit from her background.*

Let's say you don't see any common themes in your PAVES. That's okay. Some people are really good at synthesis – the ability to see patterns where others see only randomness. This is a good opportunity to ask a few close friends to look at your PAVES and ask them to help you identify commonalities and themes.

Another trick is to use a word cloud engine like Tagxedo [09] or Wordle [10] to point out the recurring themes for you. For this, complete your PAVES on a computer and then copy and paste the text into the software. Using the PAVES above, we got the visualization below. You'll note that the largest words coincide with the themes we identified.

Please keep your PAVES handy and your themes in mind. We are about to do another PAVES on your various jobs to ferret out what created meaning for you in the different places you have worked. Doing this will help distinguish what makes you different from others, and we will later use that difference as an angle to set you apart in a positive way from your competitors.

09   www.tagxedo.com

10   www.wordle.net

Focus on Your Benefits

"Humans are not ideally set up to understand logic. They are ideally set up to understand stories."

– ROGER C. SHANK, COGNITIVE SCIENTIST

exercise 06
P.A.V.E.S (YOUR WORK)

Just as with the previous exercise, create another sheet with six sections. At the top, write down the name of the last meaningful job you held or project you worked on, and then answer these questions:

•   What were you most Passionate about – if anything – in this job? Were you ever excited about your work or the promise of that work? What about that inspired you? Think really hard about this, even if it's a job you hated. Ex: My first "real job" was washing dishes at Au Bon Pain when I was 16. I hated it. But you know what? I had this weird thing for making sure the kitchen area was immaculate at the end of the night. I was a perfectionist when it came to cleanup. So for that job, "maintaining a spotless environment" would be a passion. If I can come up with a passion for this job, surely you can come up with one too.

•   What did you Accomplish in that job? What do you feel proud of? What would you brag about if you were a braggart? What made you think, "Damn, I'm good!" Maybe you wrote a report that got noticed by top management, or maybe you eradicated an entire poppy field in Afghanistan (as a friend of ours did while deployed). Whatever it is, write it down. Ex: I worked at MTV – an admin job that I also did not enjoy – but I loved coordinating everything that had to do with talent. I organized their completely insane talent acquisition system in about two weeks. That would qualify as an Accomplishment. Bringing order to chaotic systems.

•   What did you Value about that job? Was it helping people who would otherwise have been lost without you? Was it giving a perspective that no one else had? Was it simply being able to go into an office and interact with others? Ex: When I worked at the World Bank in Washington, DC, I loved all of the conversations about politics and development. I valued the feeling that I was using my gifts to make the world a better place. [11]

---

11   It is highly debatable whether the World Bank and IMF actually do help countries, and discussions like those are things I value.

- What Experiences did you collect while on that job? Did you work with interesting people or go to new places? Launch a new concept or streamline business processes? This is an easy category because you can simply jot down what you did in this section. Ex: Just as I did when I taught business in India, I have loved getting to know people and their cultures in every new place I have lived. I learned to speak to small and large audiences and feel totally at ease.

- What Skills did you acquire or share in this job? Was it clandestine human intelligence, designing jaw-dropping PowerPoints and Keynotes, programming in a new language, or managing small groups of very difficult people? Write down what you learned or – if you are expert in something – what you shared.

- Finally, what have you done professionally that you would prefer to never do again? Ex: I once had a job that was mostly about using my weak points (math and statistics) to get things done. That goes into the **Trash Can!**

If you do PAVES for each of your significant jobs, you should have a lot of red meat for your résumé, cover letter and interviews. The more detailed your answers, the more ammo you'll have for your résumé and speaking points. Compare what you've written to the content on your old résumé. Is it similar? What overlaps and what doesn't? Do you see any recurring themes in the new content you've generated?

The great thing about PAVES is that it works for all jobs and all career paths. Blue collar, white collar, no collar. Doesn't matter.

All work has value and, therefore, can be framed to demonstrate *your* intrinsic value.

Did you become an expert ice cream scooper who felt incredibly proud of creating perfectly spherical slabs of delight? Maybe you're a perfectionist who believes that delight is in the details. Does that mean you are someone who will go to great lengths to create the perfect customer experience? That quality has a lot of applications for a lot of businesses.

ALL WORK HAS VALUE AND, THEREFORE, CAN BE FRAMED TO DEMONSTRATE YOUR INTRINSIC VALUE.

At the other end of the spectrum, did your creativity and disregard for tradition allow you to completely reimagine and re-engineer an operational issue and streamline processes? Did you rid the company of layers of useless processes and paperwork? Maybe you detangled bureaucratic messes. Who doesn't love that?

 Jot it all down.

So what?

Now that you have great content for telling the story of your work history, it's important to reconsider your passions, accomplishments, values, experiences and skills through this filter: "Why should anyone care about what I've done?" Or, in other words, "So what?"

 For reference, take a look at our friend JP's resume.
(We've anonymized key content of course)

Did you make it all the way through the résumé? Really? We were bored just typing it, so it's okay if you didn't read it all. It was uninteresting because it didn't have traction. It is a vomiting of tasks and activities without attaching any purpose to them. (Notice all our "So What?s" throughout the resume.)

Imagine instead that your work accomplished something important.

JP'S RÉSUMÉ

Duties:

Currently Strategic Sourcing Manager of Company X for Customer Unit Y: Country 1, 2, 3, 4, and 5. Based in A Very Big City, I am in charge of coordinating supplier selection and contract negotiation. *SO WHAT?*
- Manage procurement activities, to secure that the business, project and commercial requirements are met, according to defined sourcing strategies and guidelines. *SO WHAT?*
- Core area of expertise involves hotels, cars, insurance, travel services, airlines, entertainment, real estate, insurance, logistics services, PR services, telecom and other business services related to proper office functioning *SO WHAT?*
- In charge of evaluating suppliers in Industry Z as well as to lead improvements of the procurement process. *SO WHAT?*
- Interact with stakeholders in 6 local companies of the region.
SO WHAT?
- Host improvement meetings with suppliers and internal stakeholders to foster standardization of Strategic Sourcing processes, and full use of Strategic Sourcing work instructions
SO WHAT?
- Participate in Regional Sourcing Process meetings and Governance Model meetings
- Local reference in the customer unit for sourcing and purchasing information
SO WHAT?

Knowledgeable in:

- Strategic Sourcing Business Processes
SO WHAT?
- Price and Contract negotiation with suppliers (hotels, car rentals, insurance, consulting companies, airlines, event organization, fit-out, printing, real estate, telecom, PR services)
- Supplier performance assessment
SO WHAT?
- In-House Finance and Banking activities *SO WHAT?*
- Cross-country treasury activities *SO WHAT?*
- International General Accounting and Finance procedures
- SAP MUS P12 (Certified), SAP P06 HRMS (Certified), SAP P36 and SAP P50 Business Warehouse
- Concur technologies, Global and Local Travel & Expense policies

Project Experience:

- Participated in the migration of Accounting Services for Market Units X and Y (2007-8)
- Led the implementation of Concur CES support in Sourcing Support X (2008-9)
- Led the migration of Sourcing Support services for X from A to B (2010)
- Led the migration and implementation of Concur CTE in Sourcing Support X in Another Very Big City.
- Participated in the implementation of Travel & Expenses services in Sourcing Support Center Country (2010)

Training Experience:

- Designed a Sourcing Training program for Sourcing Support center in three areas.
- Trained Sourcing Support Center agents in Finance, Sourcing, and Travel & Expenses service support and processes (20 agents, 3 specialists trained since 2008)
- Trained Sourcing Support Center Country agents in Concur and T&E global policies as part of the implementation of Travel & Expenses support services (2 specialists trained)
- Provided Concur training to employees at Company, Country (100 employees trained)

What if you don't know if you've ever done something important? What if you don't know how to connect what you do with what is important? We have a solution for you.

Meet The Benefit Mill.

(This space is left blank so you can start jotting down the benefits you deliver.
Because your benefits are what get you hired.)

Making a contribution, serving a larger purpose, sacrificing for x, excelling, participating in a cause (green, save the children, sustainable x, reduction/elimination of y), innovation, customer first, think differently, harmony, people development, locally-sourced, loyalty, diversity, inclusion, fair play, team spirit, flexibility

Increased sales/market share, developed new revenue streams/found new markets, decreased churn/turnover, zaccelerated growth, achieved more with same or fewer resources, made $, saved $, increased sales or profits, managed a budget well, *lowest total cost, lowest cost of ownership, ROI, ROA, profitability, up/cross-selling*

Introduced *strategic change management*, implemented vision, successfully managed the merger of x, changed aspects of corporate culture through _____ , balanced _____ excellence with meaningful growth opptys, contributed to the success of my virtual team by_____ , collaborated with peers to share knowledge, supported quality & execution, contributed to design, identified people's strengths & weaknesses, developed team through coaching & feedback, built confidence within team, influenced x, elected x of y club, managed # of employees, retained highest performers, actively looked for ways to mentor employees that were not direct reports, created a productive and satisfying team envt, managed x or y workgroups/projects, *trusted thought partner/advisor*

Increased social media followers from x to 10x, created or managed social media content, promoted X, created campaign for X, earned media, authored papers, secured/maintained global position, created IP, created or maintained a social media profile/ strategy/presence/blog, organized trade shows

REVENUE
+ / –

VALUES

BRAND +

THE BENEFIT MILL
for Résumés

LEADERSHIP

**EFFICIENCY +
WASTE –**

CUSTOMERS

RISK –

Increased efficiency, reduced waste/downtime/operating costs, eliminated redundancy, improved processes, managed x better, innovated work flows, accomplished x for the first time, developed/created/designed/architected x, managed departments efficiently, made decisions with increased speed & less pain, created tools/methodologies, decreased gaps

Understood/anticipated/responsive to customer needs, built intimacy, tailored x, customized y, exceeded company expectations under difficult or unusual circumstances, solved difficult problems, translated client requests into logical design, led a diagnostic dialogue with clients leading to business and learning outcomes, *reliability, trust, intimacy, post-purchase satisfaction*

Reduced liability/exposure, established a safety record, removed headache, identified problems others didn't see, managed conflict, responded quickly to threats, capitalized on opportunities, trustworthy, dependable, low initial investment, *past experience reduces risk of future failure or derailing*

Buzz words in italics

Our entire lives we've been trained to enter into a résumé what we've done.

"I've done this! I've done that! Look at me!" Lines on a résumé touting what you've done can also be called **feature statements.**

Everyone puts feature statements on their résumé. What most people don't think about is, "So What?" In other words, what's the benefit of you "speaking Mandarin Chinese," "managing a team of 3 people," "writing a proposal for a new product extension" or any of the other accomplishments people list on their résumés?

When you say what you did, you are talking about the past. When you say why it matters, you are talking about impact. Now, and in the future.

Guess which matters more to a potential employer.

By answering the "So What?" you turn your feature statement ("I can speak Mandarin Chinese") into a benefit statement ("With me, you will have access to the local Chinese market"). After all, it's human nature to care more about what something can do for you (benefit) than what it actually is (feature).

If you take this extra step of framing what you've done as why it matters that you've done it, you'll make it easier for a potential employer to imagine what you could do for them. You'll make it easier for them to find common ground between their needs and your ability to help them.

exercise 07

THE BENEFIT MILL

Each of the 8 core benefits of the Benefit Mill shown here is a potential filter that can convert your feature statement (what you did) into a benefit statement (why it mattered).

Pick one line from your current résumé and ask yourself, "By doing this…"

- *Did I increase revenues for my company or client?*
- *Did I increase positive brand sentiment/brand recognition?*
- *Did I increase efficiency?*
- *Did I reduce risk?*
- *Did I lead change?*
- *Did I satisfy customers?*
- *Did I demonstrate team and organizational leadership?*
- *Did I help my company meet its corporate values?*

Hopefully, what you did contributed in some way to at least one of these benefits. Do you see how there is usually more to what you did than "what you did?" You want to showcase the impact of what you did.

For example, when we ran some fairly typical feature statements from our friends' résumés, this is how they evolved as feature/benefit statements:

ORIGINAL RÉSUMÉ STATEMENTS AND PROFESSIONAL PAVES	1ST RUN THROUGH BENEFIT MILL	2ND RUN THROUGH BENEFIT MILL
I am a hardworking self-starter.	**Using Team & Org Leadership, Efficiency, and Leading Change filters:** Recognized an opportunity to improve work flows by retooling the processes of our day-to-day tasks and sales techniques.	**Using Team & Org Leadership, Efficiency, Leading Change, and Customer Satisfaction, filters:** Recognizing an opportunity to improve workflows, I retooled our daily tasks and sales techniques. This decreased processing time for new claims while increasing customer satisfaction.
I streamlined the purchase process.	**Using Revenues and Efficiency filters:** Increased sales (by 30%) and efficiency by streamlining internal processes, making it easier for customers to buy.	**Using Revenues, Efficiency, and Satisfying Customers as filters:** Streamlined the purchase process, making it easier for customers to buy and delighting them in the process, to the tune of a 30% sales increase.

I created a promotional video.	**Using Revenues filter:** Produced a promotional video for a conference that led to an increase in sales leads.	**Using Revenues, Increase Brand Recognition and Lead Change filters:** Produced a product demo that injected an established brand with a fresh sensibility, creating conference-wise buzz and converting 80% of attendees to warm leads for sales.
I successfully managed 5 people.	**Using Team & Org Leadership filter:** Built and managed a team of 5 people with the goal of turning colleagues into collaborators.	**Using Team & Org Leadership and Reducing Risk filters:** Built a collaborative team of 5, managing for cohesion, with 100% retention rate in a department with notoriously high turnover.
I trained 20 customer service agents and 3 specialists.	**Using Leading Change and Efficiency filters:** Led company to two-fold faster adoption of new finance, travel, expense and service support procedures, increasing the efficiency of over 20 agents and specialists.	**Using Increase Revenues/Decrease Costs filter:** Saved company 18% in sourcing costs by training over 20 agents and specialists in record time to permanently adopt new Finance, Travel & Expenses, and Service Support processes.
I collaborated with stakeholders in 6 countries.	**Using Corporate Values:** Promoted the company's core values of respect, professionalism, and perseverance through interactions with stakeholders in 6 countries.	**Using Corporate Values, Efficiency, and Demonstrating Team & Org Leadership filters:** Enhanced stakeholder relations across 6 countries by actively promoting the company's core values of respect, professionalism and perseverance in all interactions.

Now, run the original bullet points of your résumé and the PAVES of your past jobs through the Benefit Mill at least once. Push yourself to really consider the impact of your actions. We suggest that you consider the collateral and direct affects of what you did, not just what you directly did (your actions) in a vacuum. Don't be modest and don't exaggerate.

ORIGINAL RÉSUMÉ STATEMENTS AND PROFESSIONAL PAVES	1ST RUN THROUGH BENEFIT MILL	2ND RUN THROUGH BENEFIT MILL

If you just did what we asked – turned your feature statements into feature/benefit statements – guess what? You've just written the bulk of your résumé. Nice work!

Go celebrate with an ice cream, a latte or a walk with the dog and then come back to this book. Seriously. Go reward yourself. We'll wait.

IT IS NOT JUST WHAT YOU SAY: IT IS HOW YOU SAY IT. IF YOU TAKE ON THE PERSPECTIVE OF THE LISTENER, YOU HAVE A BETTER CHANCE THAT THE LISTENER WILL PAY ATTENTION.

JASON FINDS HIS THEMES

After Jason completed his PAVES, he saw clear recurring themes. His professional Accomplishments were in marketing. His personal Passions and Interests lay largely in athletics. And in terms of industry Experience, he had a strong background in consumer goods and apparel. With the Benefit Mill, he quantified how he had harnessed those PAVES to benefit his previous employers.

So what happened when he got a lead on a position for marketing manager at an athletic apparel company? Jason did his homework and discovered that this employer's key strength was in their customization processes for athletic apparel. Their weakness was their lack of a polished, consumer-ready brand. Their opportunity was in growing a new direct-to-consumer business. And their major threat came from low-quality, low-cost competitors.

(continued on page 69)

exercise 08
SET YOURSELF APART

This next step is about organizing your feature/benefit statements so that they make sense as a whole. Why does this matter? Have you ever talked to a 4 year old about a movie they saw? It goes like this:

And then he saved her but she was strong so strong...

and they played and blew up balloons...

then the dragon ride happened but

before that Donkey knew he liked her.

And then everyone danced. [12]

If you don't clearly connect all of the points you are trying to make, things can get confusing. You lose focus. With a résumé it's the same thing. A great résumé has focus. A great résumé tells a story. Something memorable and compelling that sets you apart from the competition, inspires someone to set an interview with you, love what you have to say, and hire you.

The recurring themes of your résumé and your P.A.V.E.S. are a clue to your story.

---

12   You knew that the four year old was describing the first Shrek ™ movie, right?

A GREAT RÉSUMÉ TELLS A STORY.

Jason matched his PAVES against the needs he deduced from this employer's SWOT. He could immediately see and prove he was the perfect match. His three key connection points were actually in the job description:

1. Marketing

They were a small but growing organization. They needed someone in marketing who could handle everything from market research to copy writing, and had direct-to-consumer experience. He had filled various marketing roles for 4 different direct-to-consumer companies, from brand strategy to campaign execution. Furthermore, he had created from scratch the branding and marketing of his own successful bakery. Though "bakery" might seem irrelevant, this entrepreneurial Achievement was actually a proof point for a company looking for an entrepreneurial self-starter that could spearhead marketing ventures into new markets and categories.

2. Athletics

In addition to coaching girl's volleyball, Jason was an avid competitor in volleyball,

(continued on page 70)

There is, however, a world of difference between telling someone your story and having them understand your story the way you intended.

Between

What I think

What I could say

What I want to say

What I believe I should say

What I say, and

What you want to hear

What you hear

What you believe you understand

What you want to understand and

What you actually understand

exist 10 possibilities for miscommunication.

- ANONYMOUS

The truth is that most people are not great listeners and would rather find something in common with you rather than really try to "get" what you are saying. In particular, interviewers have one thing on their mind when interviewing: "What can you do for me?"

Our recommendation to you: make sure that you articulate at least one clear, distinguished point that will set you apart

distinguished benefits

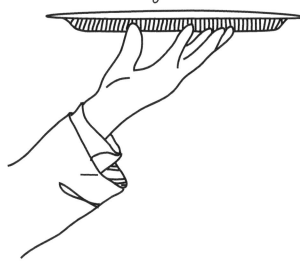

in the mind of the person interviewing you. Something they will actually hear. Something that will stick.

Remember those PAVES – both professional and personal – that you wrote down for exercises 5 and 6? Take another look at them, along with your feature/benefit statements. Do any of your personal PAVES have a possible benefit to your next employer? Do you see any recurring patterns between the work you've done and the interests you hold? Any overlap or similarities between your feature/benefit statements?

For example, we had a friend who realized that in nearly all of her previous jobs (professional) and volunteer activities (personal) she had taken on the toughest projects that no one else wanted to tackle. As a matter of fact, she liked the toughest jobs, the orphan tasks from which everyone else fled. To us, this sounded absolutely horrible. But can you imagine being a hiring manager? In walks a woman who says she likes taking on the tasks that seem too daunting or unpleasant to everyone else. And she has the professional and personal examples to prove it. To that hiring manager, she sounds like a dream. As a matter of fact, she holds out the promise of solving their greatest headaches. And for that reason, we dubbed her the Human Aspirin. That is her story. It neatly sums up the common thread between some of her most distinguished feature/benefit statements and PAVES. Best of all, it's clear and memorable.

tennis, running and CrossFit. As an Ohio State alum, he was also a rabid NCAA fan. These "interests" were no longer a footnote at the bottom of his résumé. They were germane to his ability to talk the talk in a corporate culture focused on the athletic marketplace, especially one that wanted to expand their presence in the college market. This Passion would also allow him to speak authentically to a sports-minded target customer through media, catalogues and promotions.

3. Apparel

He had worked for a major national apparel manufacturer and had direct Experience in the cutthroat retail industry. He knew the ins and outs of retail apparel, a notoriously fickle and challenging industry.

If Jason were a lawyer, we'd say he was building an airtight case for why he was uniquely qualified for this position.

For another example, let's look at an Accomplishment I listed on my PAVES: "extensive travel and living abroad." Does this set me apart? Hardly. But if I look at my Accomplishments and Experiences, as well as my feature/benefit statements, there is an obvious and recurring theme of my working in the developing world. Through the lens of the Benefit Mill's "Reduce Risk" (a benefit), this generic concept becomes something powerful.

If someone in London hires me to do employee training across their global offices in Istanbul, Madrid, Jakarta, and Bogota, they will sleep well knowing that I have a proven track record managing things in developing markets. Communicating in different languages? Check. I can speak a few languages well and can make myself understood in a few others. Eating (and even relishing) local food and customs while not getting sick? Check. Living in India and Mexico taught me how, and sharing a meal with peers (without being squeamish) is often integral in assimilating with local cultures. Building trust and rapport with Pakistanis, Brazilians, Germans, Emirates, and Thais? Check. The meeting hall is missing a door, the setup is all wrong, and the tech equipment doesn't work? BTDT. I'll adapt and make it work, so there's no stressful feedback to the planner. And so on.

All of this is about being adaptive, flexible and resourceful in the most challenging of environments and having the track record to prove it. Together, these benefits add up to a huge relief for an employer.

Imagine you are a program director or human resources planner who often hires people based on content mastery and high scores on teaching evaluations, and then deploys them internationally. How many of even the "best" candidates (per their test scores) can actually be sent to and thrive almost anywhere in the world? When someone who doesn't have my type of background sets out to do the same job, they may end up spending a lot of energy adjusting to the culture in which they find themselves and to the people whom they teach. Couple that with a naïveté about how things work in the developing world, and you might get one frustrated trainer, unsatisfied students, and a lot of wasted time and effort (i.e. money) for the employer.

It's now clear that if I want the potential employer or client to pay attention to me, it's my job to let them know that my track record of being adaptive, flexible and resourceful in the most challenging of environments makes me a superior candidate. It increases efficiencies and possibly decreases costs. But it's up to me to tell that story and make that connection for them. And if I need to sum it up for them, I'd say I'm the Chameleon. I can blend in anywhere.

We bet that if you look hard enough you'll be able to spot what sets you apart. Here's how: Review your feature/benefit statements and your PAVES .

 Identify at least three examples where two or more of your feature/benefit statements or PAVES share something in common.

These are potential themes for the story of your résumé, the things that just might set you apart from the competition. List them here:

Theme 1 _____

Theme 2 _____

Theme 3 _____

From Wendeline's examples, we get:

Theme 1: *Broad exposure to people and cultures through International Travel*

Theme 2: *Self-reliance and resourcefulness*

Theme 3: *Confidence and ability to build intimacy with strangers*

CONNECT THE DOTS

If you've done all of the exercises so far, you have a list of your personal and professional PAVES, and you've translated those into both features and benefits. You might even have a better sense of what makes your work uniquely yours in terms of recurring themes.

Now go back to exercise 3 where you did a SWOT of a dream employer. Go through the strengths, weaknesses, opportunities and threats you identified. Can you identify at least 3 areas of this employer's need that can be addressed by your PAVES?

List those three connection points here:

1. _____

2. _____

3. _____

When Wendeline was looking at working for Duke Corporate Education, she noticed these 3 connection points:

- Desire for Diversity, International Experience and Expertise

- Educators share the values of the organization

- Must keep clients happy

For each connection point, list 3 feature/benefit statements or PAVES that proves you have accomplished something related. (If you can find at least one nonprofessional proof point for each connection point, that's even better).

1. ....
2. ....
3. ....

Wendeline identified these feature/benefit statements as proof that she could deliver on the needs of Duke Corporate Education:

- *Taught in and built a professional network across 5 continents and 21 countries.*

- *Published paper on topics I taught, expanding the reach and profile of my*

  employer's brand.

- *Received excellent evaluations and remain in contact with many former students*

- *Developed new business through building intimacy and trust with clients.*

Do you realize what you just did? You've just connected the dots for a potential employer. If you were called into a surprise job interview, this very minute, you'd have three compelling things to discuss, complete with proof points. Well done. You've reduced risk for the person interviewing you and made their job easier by giving them a clearer story as to why you're the right candidate.

You can apply this methodology to match yourself to other potential positions or clients and in the next step we are going to do just that.

Find the Right Match

"What is well-conceived is easily spoken."

- VOLTAIRE

You've come a long way from that résumé you started with, haven't you? Again, we don't believe the traditional résumé is the end-all-be-all of the modern job hunt. This is especially true given, LinkedIn, Glass Door, and other career tools and sites that don't confine you to a one- or two-page document. But your résumé is useful as a foot in the door with a prospective employer or client, talking points for an interview, and an outline for your online bio.

In this section, we are going to rebuild your résumé and help you leverage it in pursuit of a real job that you want to pursue.

First, let's get to work on making your résumé interesting. Yes, we said interesting. Whether you want to admit it or not, your résumé is a marketing document. You're marketing You.

exercise 10
REBUILDING YOUR RÉSUMÉ

Imagine your résumé is the cover of a magazine at a newsstand. All of the other job hunters' résumés are also magazine covers. What would catch someone's eye about your résumé and make them pick it up for a second look?

How you organize and prioritize the information in your résumé attracts or repels, clarifies or confuses the reader as to why you are a good match for a job. To design your ideal résumé, grab a stack of sticky notes. If you prefer to work on screen, open up a blank document and get ready to do a lot of cut and paste.

Step 1

First things first. Start with the 3 typical résumé headers:

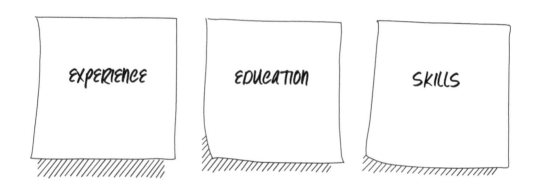

If you have published articles, then make that a 4th category, "Publications." If you have so many publications that they will not fit on the one or two pages of your résumé, then put "see attached page" under "Publications." Your stickies should read as follows:

- *Experience*

- *Education*

- *Skills/Interests*

- *Publications (optional)*

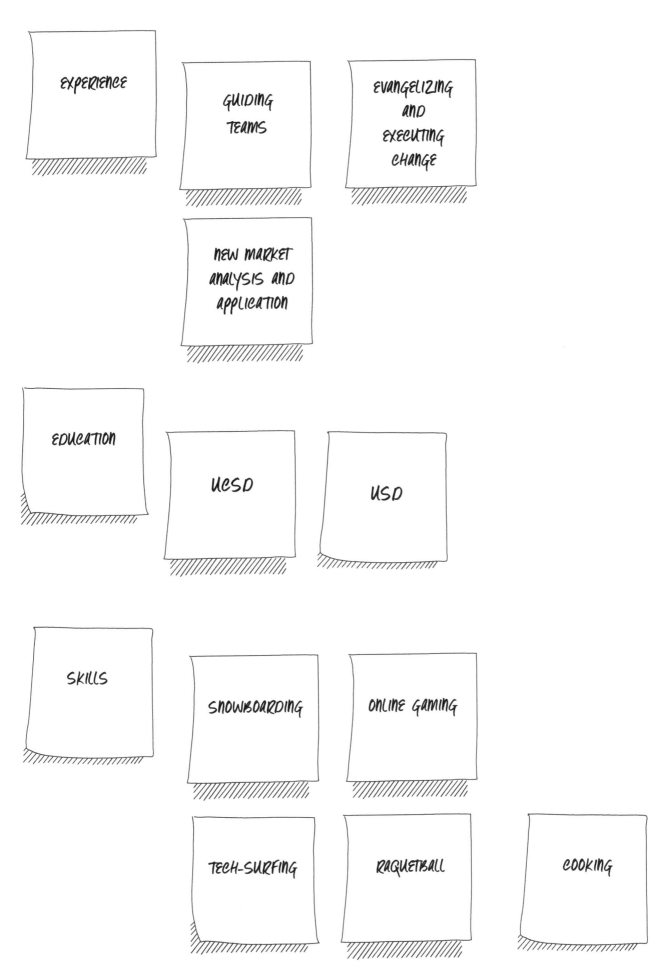

For all intents and purposes, the Experience section is the meat/main course of your résumé and it's where things can get really interesting.

There are generally three different ways you can organize or structure the experience section of your résumé. What you choose depends on where you are in your career, the job for which you're applying, and what you want to emphasize. [13]

1) Chronological – A great choice if you have a fluid and consistent career progression. List the jobs you've held starting with the most recent and ending with ancient history. This is the most common and easiest way to lay out your résumé. It can also be the least useful way of conveying information.

To do this, simply write a sticky for each job you've held (just the company name or job title is fine) and put them in order from newest to oldest.

2) By Industry – If you want to impress a potential client or employer with your knowledge about certain industries or business verticals, [14] you may want to organize your feature/benefit statements this way.

Write a sticky for each industry in which you've worked. List the jobs that fall under that industry in chronological order. If you've held different jobs at different companies, this can be a great way to create order from chaos. For example, did you work at three different restaurants and three different clothing stores over the last several years? Then maybe you're better served talking about your work in the "hospitality" and "retail" sectors to demonstrate consistency and depth of experience within those areas. Or maybe you've worked with a series of tech start-ups in a variety of positions? What do those start-ups have in common? If it's "mobile apps," "e-banking" and "intranet solutions," then you are making a strong case for

---

13 Structuring your résumé is deciding the order or how things go. Formatting it means dealing with the appearance – fonts, margins, infographics and such.

14 Verticals are certain segments of industry like retail, agriculture, direct to consumer sales, b2b marketing, etc.

leveraging that expertise for a financial services company looking to create a mobile software solution.

3)   By Skill Sets or Position – If you are gunning for work that places a heavy premium on specific skills or a group of skills, perhaps it's useful to organize around these. Examples would include supply chain management, customer service, sales, etc. Like option #2, this allows you to make sense of a series of jobs that might otherwise seem unrelated.

Write a skill set for each skill set or position type and then put the corresponding jobs with each.

Take a moment to consider what would sell you the best.

If you are not sure which type will work best for you, start with chronological and adapt from there as the picture becomes clearer. For the professional freelancer, organizing your résumé by industry or skill set can be extremely beneficial for making sense out of all your past work

Step 3

Put each feature/benefit ("f/b") statement on a sticky and lay them out underneath the different category headings under which they belong.

Move these around until you think each f/b statement is in the right place.

If you organize your résumé by skill sets or position, consider subcategorizing your work experience like this:

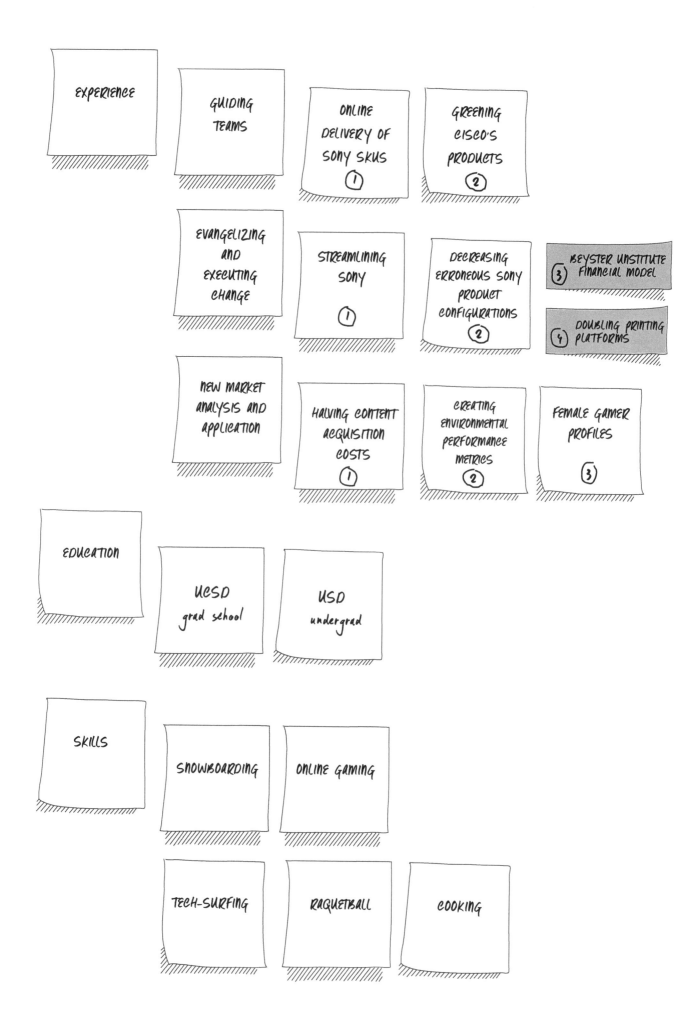

EXPERIENCE

GUIDING TEAMS

ONLINE DELIVERY OF SONY SKUS ①

GREENING CISCO'S PRODUCTS ②

EVANGELIZING AND EXECUTING CHANGE

STREAMLINING SONY ①

DECREASING ERRONEOUS SONY PRODUCT CONFIGURATIONS ②

③ BEYSTER INSTITUTE FINANCIAL MODEL

④ DOUBLING PRINTING PLATFORMS

NEW MARKET ANALYSIS AND APPLICATION

HALVING CONTENT ACQUISITION COSTS ①

CREATING ENVIRONMENTAL PERFORMANCE METRICS ②

FEMALE GAMER PROFILES ③

EDUCATION

UCSD grad school

USD undergrad

SKILLS

SNOWBOARDING

ONLINE GAMING

TECH-SURFING

RAQUETBALL

COOKING

Experience

Skill or Position A (e.g. Leading Teams)

- Active verb + direct object (feature), which resulted in x benefit to the employer.
- Active verb + direct object (benefit), by doing x, y, and z

Skill or Position B (e.g. Managing Projects)

- Active verb + direct object (feature), which resulted in x benefit to the employer.
- Active verb + direct object (benefit), by doing x, y, and z

Skill or Position C (e.g. Innovating Processes)

- Active verb + direct object (feature), which resulted in x benefit to the employer.
- Active verb + direct object (benefit), by doing x, y, and z

Experience

ACTIVE VERBS

DIRECT OBJECT/FEATURE

Creative Campaign Manager

- Developed and deployed HP brand architecture re-haul across 100 countries, resulting in a cost-effective policy that unified HP's 70-year old brand story.

Step 4

Prioritize your f/b statements. To do this, mark the f/b statements within each category that you think either

- Make the strongest statement about the benefits you bring to the table or
- Capture your greatest accomplishments or
- Differentiate you the most

You want to organize your f/b statements so that the most compelling content is at the top (i.e. most likely to be read and thus will encourage the reader to keep reading). You also want to make sure that each bullet flows from one to the next, and tells a complete story of the work you did for that company, in that industry or reflects that skill set.

Step 5

Look at the sticky note skeleton of your résumé and ask yourself "Is it well structured? Does it make sense? Does it flow?" If so, type everything into a document without worrying about perfect formatting. We're about to get to that.

If it doesn't quite feel right, move those sticky notes around until they tell a story that's persuasive. Try one of the other ways of organizing your Experience. Re-prioritize your f/b statement. Find the combination that you think puts you in the strongest light. Not sure? Ask a friend or colleague to give you feedback.

Have you done all five steps?

Wow! Guess what?

You have now outlined a great résumé. It's organized, it's prioritized, it's compelling and it's focused on the benefits you delivered to past employers and clients with the promise that you can do the same again for someone else. Nice work!

We took our good friend Josh through a similar exercise and he decided to organize his résumé around his skill sets. This helped him make sense of a very diverse work history and showcase key skills for which he knew his dream employer was looking.

We are not suggesting that your résumé should look like this. This is merely an example of how one person communicated their professional background. Your résumé should reflect your style and convey your value as clearly as possible. Check our appendix for other examples of great résumés we love. (You'll also find some other goodies there.)

Formatting your résumé

Though we are much more concerned with the content of your résumé, formatting is important, too. A well-formatted résumé guides the reader to the key points you want them to read. Here are a few tips for structuring and formatting your résumé:

Objective Statements. As we mentioned earlier, if you really, really, really want to have a mission or objective statement…then make sure it does two things:

1)   Communicates how the employer will benefit from your experience instead of saying what you seek from them

2)   Uses language that sets you apart from the competition. In the example below, we use words like "sticky" and "energizing."

We like this objective statement:
Engaging educator who receives consistently high evaluations for creating sticky content, driving high retention and energizing audiences.

But not so much this one:
Seeking a position to use my language skills and propensity for travel.

JOSH SMITH

Technology evangelist with a passion for evolving products and processes beyond the obvious. Blends market and competitive analyses with customer empathy to reimagine product requirements, and then leads teams to tactically deliver on the strategic vision.

Engineering Coordinator	Project Manager Mfg. Engineering	Market Research Analyst	Team Lead: DfE Strategy	Management Consulting	Consultant
Hewlett-Packard	**Sony Electronics**	**Sony Online Entertainment**	**Cisco Systems**	**Beyster Institute**	**Tapioca Mobile**
Mar. '04-Mar. '05	Mar. '05-Apr. '06	Spring '07	Summer '07	Oct. '07-June '08	Spring '08

EXPERIENCE

Guiding Teams

- Ensured on-time launch of 30+ Sony VAIO notebook SKUs by garnering project plan buy-in from a diverse set of stakeholders, mediating cross-functional team conflicts, and actually building the preproduction units.

- Bridged communication divide between engineering and marketing teams by crystallizing the vision for the project, working with individual team members to define research plans, and synthesizing findings into final documentation, all in an effort to insert "green" into the DNA of Cisco's products.

Evangelizing and Executing Change

- As the newest team member, identified and resolved the "elephant-in-the-room" issue that had bottlenecked the Sony VAIO team's change management process. Eliminated process redundancies, streamlined approval mechanisms and added checks and balances to create accountability. This generated cross-functional cooperation in the short-term and laid the groundwork for long-term team efficacy.

- Decreased by 65% the erroneous product configurations passed from Sony's B2B ordering system to the production floor by redesigning business processes, shortening build and rework time.

- Created a robust and enduring financial model for the Beyster Institute by redesigning their previous model around client needs and standardizing patchwork programming. This resulted in a 25% decrease in financial model completion time.

- Doubled number of printer platforms I administered within six weeks of joining HP's IPG customization team by developing a standardized process for translating GBU requirements into a logical bill of materials in SAP.

New Market Analysis and Application

- Halved projected video content acquisition costs by matching Tapioca Mobile's programming needs with video bloggers creating content. This was achieved by defining and segmenting video bloggers based on a 5-factor model using a combination of email interviews, living amongst the vloggers online, and secondary research.

- Translated Cisco's customer requirements with RoHS and other global regulations into environmental performance metrics for Cisco's core products, providing a way for engineers to design future-resistant products.

- Improved Sony Online Entertainment's understanding of the female gamer by developing in-game behavioral profiles that provided the insight for developers to increase game stickiness (retention) and for marketers to boost ad targeting (adoption).

EDUCATION

University of California, San Diego
Rady School of Management
MBA, Marketing and Business Strategy, 2008
Chief Operating Officer, Rady Student Board

University of San Diego
Olin School of Business
B.A., Business Administration, Marketing, 2003
Department Honors and Dean's Scholarship, 1998-2002

INTERESTS

Snowboarding when I can get up to the mountain; online gaming when I need to recharge; tech-surfing to stay on top of the latest and greatest technology; racquetball when I can find a partner; and cooking because I may as well eat something tasty.

Your name. Make sure your name is in a larger font than the headers. Personally, we like names justified to the upper right side. Why? Just think about a hiring manager thumbing through a stack of résumés. Unless they're left-handed, they're probably going to at least pause when they see your name in that upper right hand corner.

Contact Info. Does your employer really need your home address? If not, keep it succinct: name, mobile, email. That ought to do it for most. Some employers may want to see you're local. If that's the case, throw in your city. A link to your LinkedIn profile can be helpful as well.

The 3rd section: Interests/Experiences/Skills/Miscellaneous. Use this area wisely. Yes, it's a chance to show someone you're interesting and human and well rounded. But, really, is there anyone that doesn't like "travel"? This section is a great place to highlight a personal interest or experience that might intersect with your professional life to make you a more compelling candidate. When you look at Josh's résumé (above), you'll notice that he uses his "Interests" section to accomplish 3 things: 1) show off his sense of humor, 2) demonstrate he's well-rounded, 3) affirm that he's dialed into the tech scene because staying current ("tech surfing") is actually an interest of his.

Length. In the U.S., résumés are usually one page long, even if you have done a lot of things. Employers want to capture your essence in as few sentences as possible. For this reason, résumés that are 2 pages or longer, are generally only acceptable if you have a lot of senior experience and a long work history. A separate page is also acceptable for more technical and academic positions for which you'll want to list your published works.

THE MATCH GAME

Assuming you've completed the previous 10 exercises, you now have a kick-ass résumé that makes sense of your professional background, promotes your greatest and most differentiated strengths, and clearly demonstrates the value you added to past businesses. There's just one thing left to do: match your résumé to a specific job opportunity. A real job opportunity. *Your* real job opportunity.

So, go ahead and find a posting for a job to which you'd like to apply.
We'll wait.

Print out that job description and lay it in front of you.

~~~~~~~~~

Step 1

First, review the job description and highlight the key needs and issues listed. Here's how we broke down the "needs" as written in an actual job description.

Step 2

Ask yourself, "What are they looking to be accomplished with this position?" Translate each key need into a benefit from the Benefit Mill. Rank these benefits in order of what you think are most important to the employer.

NEED
To coordinate and supervise the execution of works as well as ensure the implementation of the same with quality and compliance, meeting all deadlines.
Will also be responsible for procuring resources to meet budgetary requirements.
Preparation of monthly production and certification.
Spanish written and spoken is mandatory.
Minimum 2 years experience as a Project Manager.
Possibility of international travel, linked with contracts.

Step 3

Reconcile the key needs of the job description with the SWOT research you did for that company. (exercise 3) How important is this to their goals? Does this job description help them build on one of their strengths? Address a weakness? Capitalize on an opportunity? Battle a potential threat? Prioritize what you think are the most important issues facing this employer that this position can address.

NEED	BENEFIT
To Coordinate and supervise the execution of works as well as ensure the implementation of the same with quality and compliance, meeting all deadlines.	• Increase efficiency • Lower risk • Demonstrate Team & Organizational Leadership
Will also be responsible for procuring resources to meet budgetary requirements.	• Lower Costs • Maintain/Increase Efficiency
Preparation of monthly production and certification.	• Lower risk • Efficiency • Protect Brand Value
Spanish written and spoken is mandatory.	• Maintain/Increase Efficiency • Achieve corporate values • Lower risk
Minimum 2 years experience as a Project Manager.	• Lower risk • Maintain/Increase Efficiency
Possibility of international travel, linked with contracts.	• Decrease Costs • Increase Efficiency

You will also want to consider what is not written in the job description. If your research revealed anything specific about the company needs, add those to your list.

If you get stuck, ask yourself the following questions:

- *Why is the employer posting a job? (Who left? What changed?)*
- *What is the employer or client looking for? (as explicitly stated in job description)*
- *What do you know about their unmet needs? (as not stated in job description)*

- *How can you help them?*

- *What proof do you have that you can do that?*

- *How are you different (i.e. uniquely qualified) from other candidates that can also help them do that?*

Step 4

Since you have outlined what you think this employer needs and why, ask yourself these three questions:

1.   *Does this job still interest me? If yes, then...*

2.   *Have I ever filled a similar need?*

3.   *Have I ever done work that's created a similar benefit? (the proof)*

Match at least one f/b statement for each of their identified needs.

WHAT IS WRITTEN IN THE JOB DESCRIPTION	WHAT YOU THINK THEY ARE REALLY ASKING FOR, GIVEN THEIR SWOT	YOUR PROOF (FROM YOUR F/B STATEMENTS)
CIVIL ENGINEER, **automotive sector:** To Coordinate and supervise the execution of works as well as ensure the implementation of the same with quality and compliance, meeting all deadlines.	They need someone who can carry out projects that others have strategized already. You will have a boss and will have to meet quality and compliance standards, as well as deadlines.	

WHAT IS WRITTEN IN THE JOB DESCRIPTION	WHAT YOU THINK THEY ARE REALLY ASKING FOR, GIVEN THEIR SWOT	YOUR PROOF (FROM YOUR F/B STATEMENTS)
Will also be responsible for procuring resources to meet budgetary requirements.	You will have to know how to negotiate down prices for parts.	
Preparation of monthly production and certification.	You need to do paperwork well. This is not a get-it-done-just-in-time-and-now-there's-another-crisis-to-deal-with job.	
Spanish written and spoken is mandatory.	Certain Employees and Executives in the corporation speak only Spanish. No fudging this ability.	
Minimum 2 years experience as a Project Manager.	You must have experience in managing projects. Show this by using key words that indicate insight born from experience in the area.	
Possibility of international travel, linked with contracts.	You may travel to negotiate better deals on parts.	

Step 5

Reorganize your f/b statements so they reflect what you think are the most important needs of this position. Prioritize these key points in your cover letter, résumé, interview answers, etc. For the person reviewing your résumé, you are formulating a simple equation:

THE EMPLOYER'S NEEDS AND DESIRED BENEFITS

=

MY FEATURE/ BENEFIT STATEMENTS

JOSH'S STORY

Our friend Josh did a great job of matching his personal accomplishments with a job opportunity and distinguishing himself in the process of doing so. According to Josh's PAVES, one of his greatest accomplishments was taking apart the engine in his car without any professional training or guidance and reassembling it to make his car go faster. This was a feat that required resourcefulness, precision, ingenuity and guts. If he didn't succeed, he'd have destroyed his car. He re-engineered his car's engine, resulting in a net 4 mph faster max speed.

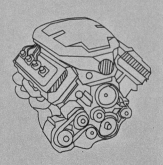

When he applied for a job at a tech firm to lead up a product team, he figured they needed someone who could drive incremental improvements, surely and steadily. When

(continued on page 95)

In the case above, it has become clear that the employer needs someone responsible and low risk to run the shop smoothly.

If you were applying for this job, you would ask yourself, "Have I ever managed a project smoothly and efficiently? Am I a responsible, detail-oriented person who can negotiate well?"

Your ability to "prove" that you can do the job you seek will help decrease their perceived risk in hiring you.

In addition to identifying Needs and Benefits, it's also helpful to make a checklist of all the basic qualifications that this employer or client has identified. Go ahead, make a checklist with a little box next to each item. How many can you check off?

Our friend Abby literally listed the key feature/benefits to her potential employer, and she did so with a measure of forthrightness and personality that set her apart. How do we know? Because the person who employed her is a past client of ours who, when they heard about this book, said, "I got the best cover letter ever. You HAVE to see this." Abby's been working with that same company ever since.

If you don't meet every single requirement for which they ask, it doesn't mean you're out of the running. It just means you have to be able to better explain why you're a superior candidate. After all, employers create a "wish list" of skills, education, and qualifications based on what they think the candidate needs to do the job exceptionally well. Maybe some requirements are more essential than others. Do you have a similar experience that proves you're capable of doing this or that you're a quick learner?

From:
Subject: **FW: USE THIS VERSION OF THE COVER LETTER.**
Date: April 21, 2010 10:27:10 AM PDT
To:
Cc:

Best. Cover Letter. Ever.

From: **ABBY JOHNSTON**
Sent:
To: Amy
Subject: USE THIS VERSION OF THE COVER LETTER.
Importance: High

Dear Potential Employer,

Attached to this document is my resume. I am sure that it looks like most of the other fifty that you will read carefully, line by line (yeah, right) on your search for something special. Resumes, in my opinion, are pretty boring. They are essentially just work histories. Okay, I have the skills to do the job. So do the other applicants. Why should you hire me?

Because I have that something special for which you seek. This letter is my first opportunity to prove it. By all means, take a look at my resume. Then, as the process requires, look at thirty more. When all of the words begin to mash together, rifle back through the pile on your desk looking for that something special. You will find me again. I am the needle in the haystack! If you hire me, you will not be disappointed. Let me give you five good reasons:

1) This is a match made in heaven. What you need is the best Project Coordinator that money can buy (me). What I need is someone who can give me a good job in an environment where I can thrive (you).

2) We both have to work for a living, so why not be as productive as possible? I guarantee that my presence in your office will increase your productivity.

3) You will never have to explain anything to me twice. I am a quick learner.

4) I am the ultimate time-saver. Tell me what you want done, and I will do it, without supervision. You never need to spend extra time wondering whether I will get the job done. I will get the job done.

5) I will go above and beyond the call of duty - just for fun.

If you give me a chance, I promise that you will NOT be disappointed!

I thank you in advance for doing something that will make us both very happy. At your earliest opportunity, please call me to discuss.

With anticipation,

ABBY JOHNSTON

Project Coordinator | Precision Dynamics International

he interviewed for the job and they asked him why he thought he was right for this, he had a very interesting story – among relevant professional accomplishments – that distinguished him as being someone who could drive incremental innovation. He was the guy that took his car engine apart in his kitchen and rebuilt it for greater speed and efficiency. This proved he was resourceful, precise, ingenious and gutsy. And it was a story that was memorable to the interviewer.

He got the job.

It is up to you to show them that you can do it, even if you don't fulfill or meet every requirement. As you dissect the job description, highlight the key words and phrases that jump out at you. Make a list of these and be sure to incorporate that same language when you communicate with the potential employer or client. Reusing keywords in your résumé, cover letter and interview will signal to the listener that you really hear them. Just don't overdo it. A few keywords is all you need to signal "I get you."

And, finally, when answering these questions, make sure that you clearly state how you are different from the competition. What makes you special? Your revised résumé – with all of its new feature/benefit statements – should have plenty of ammo for distinguishing you from the competition.

If you aren't clear on what sets you apart, go through your résumé, your PAVES, your feature/benefit statements and your themes. Imagine other job candidates are competing against you for the same job. Star the items that you think your competitors won't also say. This is what sets you apart. These are your **positive differentiators** or your **"unfair advantages"** as my high school friend, Charlie Piper, says. [15] And, thus, these should take priority in telling your story.

15 Your positive differentiators or unfair advantages are things that you have that others cannot easily copy.

IT IS UP TO YOU TO SHOW THEM THAT YOU CAN DO IT, EVEN IF YOU DON'T FULFILL OR MEET EVERY REQUIREMENT.

Speak
the truth

"You don't want to be considered just the best.
You want to be considered the only one who does what you do."

– JERRY GARCIA

"SO, WHAT DO YOU DO? TELL ME ABOUT YOURSELF."

Questions like these suck. Especially when you're in the midst of a job search or a job transition. And even more so when you're at a mixer or some incredibly awkward networking event. You can practically see the thought-bubble forming in the other person's mind as they decide whether it will be worth their time to continue the conversation. Awkward.

We're hoping that this book has better prepared you for answering this question – whether it be casually or in an interview. If you've completed the previous eleven exercises, you should now know a lot more about what you've done, about the value you provided, and how you can connect the dots to what you want to do next. In turn, you can better position these unique benefits to potential clients or employers.

Let's assume that by now your cover letter and résumé dazzle. A résumé is just a piece of paper (or a digital file), though. It's only the first step. It gets you noticed. What you really want a résumé to do is to get you the interview. Because it's when the hiring manager or the client asks you "Tell me about yourself" that it really matters.

In an interview, it's your job to tell them something about yourself that gives you a competitive advantage. Something that's interesting, authentic and memorable. Something that matters. Think of your answer as the shiny bait on the end of a fishhook that will get them to bite. Like Josh's story about dissecting his car's engine.

Figuring out the answer to this question is really about understanding how your past makes sense in light of what you want to do now and where you're headed. Or, in other words, being able to tell your story.

Instead of "Tell me about yourself," reimagine you've been asked,
"Tell me something that you've done that I might never have guessed."

Think about it. This is your chance to share something that is not pat or rote. Something they've never ever heard before in all of the interviews they've conducted. In other words, something memorable.

I could say "I am a marketing consultant," but where I live (San Diego) that's like saying "I like sunshine." It's a non-starter because practically everyone would or could say that. Instead, I could say, "I get companies to think like a movie studio." Or, "I cultivate organic vegetables and hope to build out the garden as a community garden for kids." Or, "Well, for fun, I help other people figure out what they love to do." Any of these are going to be much better departure points for a conversation.

What we want to uncover here is the essence of who you are. This part might seem a little less, well, practical. Maybe even a little airy-fairy to you. Trust us. There is a very practical reason you want a clear understanding of your unique value and be able to tell that in a compelling story.

What you are looking for is an understanding of the guiding themes in your life. In my case, when someone asks me, "What do you do?" I sometimes answer, "I help adults communicate better," or "I teach leaders how to manage their people." Those statements often draw a pause and allow me to describe with more passion what I do. I like to keep in mind Voltaire's words, "The secret to being boring is to say everything." Say enough to pique someone's interest and not more. You don't need to communicate every selling point about yourself all at once.

To come up with something meaningful, look back at your PAVES (we promised you it would pay off). Now look at your résumé. Identify the items that most excite you. Don't overthink this. Just do it.

How do your answers line up with the themes you identified in Exercise 8? Do you see any overlap? These are going to be the clues as to your life's themes. For Josh, it was about his never-ending pursuit to make things work better and faster. Can you imagine being a hiring manager whose task it is to find a product manager who will nurture the development of a product so that it continues to evolve and provide value for the company? And then in walks this guy who had the audacity to take the engine out of his car just so he could reassemble it and get 4 extra mph's out of it? This is someone you want to listen to. At least his stories will be interesting.

And great stories are integral to acing the interview. When we say "story" we don't mean make-believe. And we don't mean epics or huge calls to action either. We mean interesting examples of your accomplishments that have a clear beginning, middle, end and, importantly, the reason you brought up the example in the first place. (the benefit to the employer)

Imagine you walk into an interview room. The interviewer sits behind a desk and, without really getting up, extends her hand and says, "Nice to meet you." In her left hand, she holds your résumé, which she glances at quickly. You notice that the room is a little cold, but the seat is still warm from the person she interviewed before you. You're thinking, "How will I make myself stand out? Will I remember what I prepared for? I hope I don't come across as stupid." Or maybe you're thinking, "I can't wait to kick some serious butt here! I am perfect for this job, and they will love me!" At that moment, the interviewer asks, "What single project or task would you consider the most significant accomplishment in your career so far?"

You are floored. This is a HUGE question. "There are so many projects and tasks that were significant to me," you tell yourself. "Why does she want me to limit it to just one? How will I know which is the most significant? It may be significant to me, but maybe it wasn't determinative for the company..."

Relax. If you've done the exercises in this book your answer is buried somewhere in there, like a jewel in the form of a résumé bullet point.

Mitch found his greatest accomplishment in "Managed customer relations," which set him up to talk about an episode with a disgruntled customer that he turned into a happy customer.

For Jason, it was his unusual career detour of opening up his own gourmet bakery because in marketing parlance, this demonstrated he was able to create something from nothing, build a successful brand, and manage that brand for growth.

For me (Wendeline) it was my extensive work abroad in many countries across many cultures, which made me the ideal candidate for a company like Duke Corporate Education because they could literally send me anywhere and know that I could build alliances.

And for Josh, well, it was hard to beat his accomplishment of building that engine, which proved ingenuity, determination, resourcefulness and guts.

How do you actually talk about your accomplishments, though? How will you know you are making sense in the telling? We suggest you S.W.E.A.R. about it.

When you tell your story, make sure you articulate the following:

S   **Situation** (give just enough background for the story to make sense)

W   **Who** (tell us who is involved)

E   **Emotions** (tell us how they felt—mad, glad, sad, scared, or surprised)

A   **Actions** (tell us what they did to show how mad, glad, sad, scared, or surprised they were)

R   **Response** (tell us what you did to address the problem above and how it made you feel)

And always, tell the interviewer the Benefits to him/her/the company of the story by sharing what you learned from the incident.

For example:

*The most significant accomplishment in my career so far was when I transformed a total financial loss with a threat of a lawsuit into a super-satisfied customer who, after speaking with me, ended up purchasing more than he ever had before. **(S)** When I managed customer relations for Company X, a **(W)** customer was **(E)** so irate with our service that he **(A)** came into the office to complain. I **(R)** listened to everything he had to say without contradicting him. It was really hard because some of what he said had nothing to do with our product, but with his use of it. But because I wanted to make sure our customer was happy, I heard him out, asked him questions about how he used it, and finally, worked with our engineers to design something that made not just this customer happy but satisfied all of our customers. This is the type of person I am. One who will make sure our customers are delighted, and with that, I can help increase revenue and customer retention."*

 # S.W.E.A.R. YOUR WAY TO THE TOP

Answer this question: "What single project or task would you consider the most significant accomplishment in your career so far?"

Now, SWEAR by it. Look at your résumé. Focus on one bullet point at a time. Can you think of a specific instance that proves that point? When you find that bullet point and that story that makes you really proud, fill this in:

The Accomplishment (in one sentence) is:

Situation: _____

_____

_____

Who: _____

_____

_____

Emotions: _____

_____

_____

Actions: _____

_____

_____

Response: _____

_____

_____

Look at that. You've just answered "The most important interview question" of all time and you made it interesting.

It's important to remember that not every interviewer or potential boss will spend all of their time interviewing you about your past. Some care much more about what you want to do going forward because they want to ensure that your aspirations align with your potential job, with their aspirations (if you're working together), as well as with the company's recruitment and retention goals. The future-focused question that you are likely hear in an interview is

"Where do you see yourself in 5 or 10 years?"

Most large companies want you to stay for at least two years, if not five, and this questions gives them a chance to assess your commitment and ambition. It's their way of getting inside your head to figure out

- *How does this position fit into your personal life plan?*

- *Will this person be motivated?*

- *Will this person leave after a year?*

- *Does this person have realistic expectations?*

- *Is s/he arrogant?*

- *Did they research us properly?*

These answers to these questions fall into 3 basic buckets:

Retention. A recruiter wants you to be committed because rehiring and retraining employees is expensive, time-consuming and makes the hiring manager look bad if the new hire leaves within the first year. Employers want to believe you will stick around for a while. Never lie during an interview, but also keep in mind that you don't need to tell them about your intention to apply to law/grad school in the next two years, or that you'll bail if your band gets signed or your app gets bought. You might change your mind on the first condition and you can't predict the outcome of the first, second or third.

Mindset. They want to know you have a "can do" attitude, are not arrogant, are realistic, have some ambition, are honest, and so on, depending on who is doing the interviewing.

Do I like you? When all is said and done, people buy from or hire those they know and like. This bucket is about HOW you answer the question. There are plenty of books, websites, and training courses that can assist you here, and we will offer you some tips, but ultimately, you do not want to work for someone who doesn't like you, or in a company where you feel a cultural mismatch. You need to like the people you work with in order to be happy there, and they need to like you for them to be happy.

To answer the "Where do you see yourself in 5 years" question well, you would do well to: nv

1. Research a typical/reasonable career path that flows from the position for which you are interviewing. Go to the company website, LinkedIn, or Google—and if that doesn't work—check with people you know in similar professions and find out how many years one typically stays in the position you want. While you are there, figure out what the next position(s) is (are) on the path. Knowing this will prepare you to answer any questions about long-term intentions with the job for which you're applying.

For McKinsey & Co., their typical road map looked like this:

Business Analyst > Associate > Engagement Manager > Associate Principal > Partner

2. Speak in terms of your professional, not personal, development and goals.

    I'd like to have grown in and with the company, acquired skills beyond those I need for this

    particular position, mastered the ability to _____, exceeded the targets set out by management...

3. Emphasize the value you bring with regards to bottom line results for the business. These are the benefits listed in the Benefit Mill. For example,

    ...I want to make a positive difference to your company...securing and maintaining its global position,

    solving previously-intractable problems, contributing to success of my peers and boss, adding to the bottom

    line, eliminating inefficiencies, inspiring innovation...

    Or

    I want to have helped the company grow locally, inspired those around me, felt as if I contributed to the general

    good of this place by engaging customers more and due to that, made our company even more customer-centric

    than it already is, which will of course contribute to our shareholder value...

4. Do not speak in terms of titles or salaries. You'll just sound self-serving.

5. Let your preparation and enthusiasm shine through to demonstrate your interest in the company. You CAN be specific when it comes to their products, customers, and competition.

    In the next five years, I see myself sitting in front of you, and you are happy that you hired me because I'll

    have made this company richer through innovative products / services like (name one or some), because

    I will have created new customer needs by listening to what partners like (name current customers) are

    saying, and because I will have developed my leadership skill-set in the process of crushing our competitor, __

    _____(name it).

One last point: Some hiring managers want to know that you aspire to walk on the path they are on, and your qualifications like education and experience are simply boxes to be checked. They are much more interested in identifying your intention. What's more, many HR departments say they would rather hire for attitude and teach skills. If that's the case, your can-do attitude (and proof of it, like Joshua rebuilding his engine) could be the thing that gets you the job.

PEACE OUT.

Congratulations. You've completed all 12 exercises. You've eviscerated your résumé, discovered your P.A.V.E.S and survived the Benefit Mill. You've played the Match Game with a job description and learned to S.W.E.A.R. really, really well. Most importantly, you've resurrected your résumé so it works for you. Now it's time to get out there and put all of this effort to good use.

That's your job now. Let employers see what makes you tick. Let them understand how you are uniquely positioned to help them succeed. Give them every reason to want to keep the conversation going with you. Because once you've done that, you've made yourself a talent pool of one.

But before we go, we have one more question for you...

"SO, WHAT MAKES YOU DIFFERENT?"

Appendix

SAMPLE RÉSUMÉS

There are so many good résumés out there (no, really, there are). There are even some especially creative, fun and interesting résumés out there. Following is a small selection of résumés that a) we had permission to use and b) represented a radical departure from their original résumé before going through the Being Different Matters process; and c) actually worked. These people found the jobs for which they are looking.

For example, our friend Joe was just starting out in his career and had done a lot of retail sales. He wasn't sure how to communicate what these smaller jobs really said about the direction in which he was going.

These are his before and after résumés.

Joseph Reed

(555)-555-5555 | Joeseph@example.com

Objective

With a strong desire to maximize my creative abilities, I strive to highlight and emphasize my interpersonal skills and hard work ethic to assist in the success of an organization.

Work Experience

Bossa Nova Restaurant – Los Angeles, CA
June 2009 – December 2009 • *Server*
Only server in company trained at all four store locations.

Waltrip's Music – Arcadia, CA
April 2009 – August 2009 • *Store Manager*
Manage and maintain showroom sales, oversee and coordinate outside sales events, handle customer support and service.

Yamaha Corporation – United States
May 2008 – April 2009 • *Outside Sales Coordinator*
Managed outside sales events at Costco. Product Specialist. Educate and sell Yamaha Acoustic, Digital and Player Pianos.

Concord Music Group – Beverly Hills, CA
October 2008 – December 2008 • *VP of A&R Administrative Assistant (Temp)*
Liaise between supervisor, artists, prospective artists and their primary contacts. Screen and prioritize incoming calls. Manage demo tape submission requests. Assist artists and their contacts when able. Contract administration and standard contract templates. Process and track invoices. Burn CDs and arrange for internal and external delivery. Organize expense reports.

Emoto Music – Santa Monica, CA
April 2008 – September 2008 • *Intern*
Assisted with composing and studio engineering work. Responsible for directing phone calls. Responsible for delivering time sensitive materials. Organized and arranged lunch menus for clients. Maintained and updated client database.

Keyboard Concepts – Van Nuys, CA
February 2007 – February 2008 • *Outside Sales Coordinator*
Managed outside sales events at Costco. Trainer for sales closing techniques and product knowledge.

Original Music School – Cedar Knolls, NJ
2006 – 2007 • *Music Instructor/Assistant Engineer*
Piano and Songwriting Instructor for eight students. Assisted studio engineer with production and live tracking.

Rockaway Music – Morris Plains, NJ
2001 – 2006 • *Sales Staff Representative*
Redesigned and remarketed sales floor to increase sales. Designed magazine ads and mailing promotions to drive more customers to the store. Sold more than 100 units in one year. Responsible for setting up and maintaining computer network. Managed scheduling software. Provided technical support and resolved customer issues.

Education

Montclair State University – Montclair, NJ
2006 • B.A., Classics and Humanities. "The humanities are academic disciplines which study the human condition, using methods that are primarily analytic, critical, or speculative, as distinguished from the mainly empirical approaches of the natural and social sciences."

Belmont University – Nashville, TN
2004 • Majored in Commercial Piano and Music Business. Experienced wide instruction with both digital and analog tracking and editing in extremely high-end state of the art studios.

Computer Skills

Proficient in Macintosh and PC, Adobe Photoshop, Logic, Pro-Tools, Final Cut Pro, Reason, Outlook, FileMaker Pro, Nuendo, Microsoft Word, Excel, and PowerPoint, basic HTML and website design knowledge.

References Available upon request.

JOE REED

06/10 - PRESENT: Sales Representative, *Steinway & Sons,* Paramus, NJ
04/08 – 02/10:   Post Production Coordinator, *Emoto Music,* Santa Monica, CA
03/07 - 02/09:   Consultant, *Yamaha Corporation*, Los Angeles, CA
09/01 - 12/06:   Sales Representative, *Rockaway Music*, Morris Plains, NJ

PURPOSE:
I have over ten years of experience dealing directly with the consumer and getting them to say "yes" to extremely large ticketed items. I hope to have you say "yes" to me when I ask for a job with your company.

SALES EXPERIENCE:

I am trustworthy; therefore I currently manage over two million dollars of inventory for Steinway & Sons

I am creative, so I designed and launched the social media marketing platforms including Facebook, MeetUp and Twitter for Steinway Piano Gallery in Paramus

Since I get along well with others, I scheduled, coordinated and performed nationwide piano sale events for Yamaha Corporation leading to expanded territories and increased outside sales for dealers

I don't like to brag, but I made the single greatest piano sale in an outside sales event history for Yamaha Corporation yielding an overall number one top grossing event of all time

POST PRODUCTION EXPERIENCE: (EMOTO MUSIC)

I am able to manage my time effectively and focus all of my efforts on issues in the order of importance, so I managed, scheduled and coordinated distribution of final delivery elements such as masters, promotional spots, and clips for the publicity/marketing department to meet specific deadlines

By paying meticulous attention to details, being internet savvy and having an organized work environment, I was able to maintain client relations and arrange meetings, conference calls and travel arrangements even more efficiently by using coupon codes and online travel deals

Because I think analytically and strategically, I was able to assist in revising and maintaining databases, systems and procedures

Because I am always one hundred percent dedicated to the project I am involved with, I will often work during non-work hours and not complain about it

I contributed to a positive workplace

EDUCATION:
MONTCLAIR STATE UNIVERSITY, Montclair NJ
Bachelor of Arts, *Marketing* – 2007
BELMONT UNIVERSITY, Nashville Tennessee
Associates Degree, **Music** – 2004
MBA Degree in International Business to stat Fall 2011

SKILLS/INTERESTS:
Proficient in ProTools, Photoshop, CRM, Act!, Microsoft Office, Excel and Powerpoint
I have played piano professionally on Sunset Blvd in Hollywood California
Letters of recommendation available upon request

Education

Master of Business Administration, 2005-2007   Rady School of Management, University of California, San Diego
- Rady School Dean's Fellowship; EAT food club, founder/president; Rady Investments club, member, GPA 3.9

Bachelor of Arts, cum laude, in Economics, 2002-2005   University of California, San Diego
- Phi Beta Kappa, Dean's List, intramural captain, graduated with honors in 3 years

Experience

Hewlett Packard- Printing & Personal Systems Group, San Diego, 2008- Current   *WW Integrated Marketing Manager*
- Create, manage, deploy, and elevate comprehensive global marcomm programs from strategic briefing to execution:
    - Retail: Invoke shopper marketing insights to produce arresting content, messaging, packaging, touch point plans, and photography in complete savvy retail toolkits tailored to product/country needs. Refined demo days in big box stores to drive month over month increases in traffic and 120-150% over forecast sales.
    - Social: Develop prime target for social channels to help drive interest/feedback around products with limited shelf space. Effective posts netted most comments/feedback to date, and earned free paid promos from other groups, as well as secured HP in beta testing for new Twitter initiatives.
    - Videos: Produce on average 2 videos a month across initiatives- from brief to scripting. Utilize on hub, pan social channels, and attract loops. Top 2013 series received 6.5million views with 90% completion rate.
    - Digital: Be it static, rich, internal and paid, develop and traffic it all. Close monitoring of paid search and demand gen CTAs resulted in "most efficient" SEM campaign. Pioneered mobile first designs for sites spiking engagement rates.
    - Comms: Write internal blasts from small groups to 350k worldwide to education and excite. Externally submit monthly CRM programs to 13M. Partner with AR & PR to organize press releases, interviews & tradeshows.
    - Influencers: Engage key target advocates for each program. Act as spokesperson for TwoSmiles and with Disney mommy bloggers to increase WOM. Run webinars, coordinate posts, and incentive programs. For TV, scripted Rachael Ray and Designing Spaces segments for holiday press.
    - Admin: Run $1M+ campaign budgets, facilitate global team projects, administer research/testing, gather ROI and results, manage agency relationships and internal pitches.
    - "Connector" Role: Passion to always be internal advocate of good programs, promoting them, securing resources, and highlighting accomplishments with end goal of leveraging and extending existing work.

Chuao Chocolatier, Carlsbad, CA, 2007   *Consultant*
- Created & implemented comprehensive employee training process, manual, and standardization across 5 stores
- Refocused café experience around customer loyalty to increase sales and brand equity

General Electric- Global Electronics Services, La Jolla, CA, 2006   *Marketing Intern*
- New Product Development for Flat Panel Display: Drove market research, facilitated international communications, worked with a team to define value proposition & successfully executed strategy to pass GE toll-gate
- Sales tool kit: Initiated "voice of consumer" study to redefine sales needs & develop targeted intelligence
- Strategic Thinking: Classified & analyzed historic GES data through non-investment & investment opportunity approach. Developed strategic recommendations & comprehensive pitch to focus growth goals.

Santa Cruz County Office of Education, Santa Cruz, CA, 2003- 2004   *Administrative Assistant*
- Efficiently researched, compiled, & edited the 2002-03 Grand Jury Response Report
- Collaborated with the superintendent to revise a district-wide health & safety manual for rapid implementation
- Entered & managed payroll data for the business & financial services department

Skills

- *Systems:* Microsoft Office suite, Sharepoint design/interface, Business Warehouse GL reporting, BOSS HR systems, ThinkCell graphic software, & SmartBuy procurement system
- *English:* native language.   *American Sign Language:* conversational level.   *Spanish:* conversational level

Interests

- Events planner, organizer, and implementer –avid cook & healthy-lifestyle devotee
- Runner, surfer, hiker, yoga student & outdoor enthusiast
- Nonprofit devotee + contributor- Casa de Amistad/former Carmel Valley Homework Helper team lead, Young Employee Networks, San Diego schools, I ♥ a Clean San Diego, LSB Church, & Loaves & Fishes

This is Carrie's before.

It's impressive, to be sure, but hard to pin down exactly what she can do and wants to do.

AFTER

CARRIE CAR

Experience

Hewlett Packard
2008-Current
Global Integrated Marketing Manager
Business/Global Strategy & Creative Manager
Global Marketing Operations Manager

Chuao Chocolatier
2007
Marketing & Ops Consultant

General Electric
2006
Marketing Strategist

Marketing leadership from inception to execution across four quadrants:

- **Marketing Strategy and Optimization**
  o Worldwide strategic and creative campaign manager of HP initiatives ranging from shoestring to $10M budgets.
  o Co-developed and deployed HP brand architecture re-haul across 100 countries, in-store and online. Net result: cost effective policy to unify HP's 70 year old brand story.
  o Authored and produced Chuao's employee manual to establish operational efficiency across all of their 5 stores.
- **Opportunity Forging**
  o Pioneered live van tour and HP's first mobile text offer, bringing products to life. This increased sales by an estimated 30%, drove page growth to meet 1B goal and earned Best Guerilla Marketing Award.
  o Championed HP "blue thread" in consumer printing: singular guiding messaging playbook to establish brand consistency and clarity internally and externally.
  o Reconfigured Chuao's café incentive programs engaging customers and increasing loyalty.
  o Engaged HP's previously-neglected 13M printer-installed base with a refreshed customer e-blasts driving conversion
- **Multi-Channel Activation**
  o Retail: Produced "Best HP Toolkit" using arresting and regionally-nuanced retail point of sale plans.
  o Events: Modified HP's Ambassador Program to improve store branding resulting in 135% improvement over sales forecast.
  o Video: Produced 30+ product, training, education, and sizzle videos in last year. Top 2013 series received 6.M views with 90% completion rate.
  o Social: Strategy lead and content developer. Earned free paid promos and secured HP in Twitter beta testing.
  o Influencers: HP Media trained spokesperson, committed to securing long term interest and advocacy programs to extend impact of traditional press launches to TV/web events.
  o Digital: Activated test and learn pilots with new media channels. For example, promoted mobile-first designs, spiked engagement rates (4-5 minutes versus sub 1 minute), and achieved "most efficient" SEM campaign for HP mobile printing.
  o Fundamentals: Incorporated ROI assessments to develop TV spots, radio, and print assets to target and reach traditional customers where statistically efficient.
- **Silo-Busting & Alignment Building**
  o Identified scope overlap at HP to combine and streamline 2 competing photo systems into one, reducing cannibalization and netting one centralized hub for customers to meet multiple needs.
  o Developed system to classify non-investment of GE semi conductor businesses- to quantitatively assess new partnerships. Used this basis to apply metrics driven approach with HP beta team to efficiently uncover new offerings in ink services.
  o Implemented voice of employee program to restructure GE's traditional sales guide leading to earlier marketing and sales alignment.

Education + Skills

M.B.A. Rady School of Management 2005-2007 Marketing Emphasis Dean's Fellowship Award	B.A. in Economics U.C. San Diego 2002-2005 Cum laude, Dean's List	Languages English Spanish American Sign Language	Systems Microsoft Office, SharePoint, Business Warehouse, BOSS HR, ThinkCell, SmartBuy, Aprimo

Interests

- **Mentor and Program Lead:** 15+ year tutoring of minority to gifted students across Santa Cruz and San Diego counties
- **Nonprofit devotee:** community advocate and marketing lead: Swim24Challenge, Casa de Amistad, I ♥ a Clean San Diego, Run North County
- **Flair for:** event planning, organizing programs to clutter, cooking & running, surfing, yoga and all things outdoors

This is Carrie's résumé after doing the exercises. She makes it clear what type of work she most wants to do and why she is uniquely qualified to do it.

Ways I can change my own résumé:

MARK MALLOY

SUMMARY

Enthusiast in solving complex problems and identifying relevant, actionable opportunities. Combines experience in academic research, business, and design to drive projects and quickly build momentum. Excels in highly collaborative environments that require interpersonal skills, focus, and multidisciplinary perspectives.

SKILLS

Problem-Solving	● ● ● ● ●
Research	● ● ● ● ●
Data Analysis	● ● ● ● ○
Graphic Design	● ● ● ● ○
Programming	● ● ● ○ ○
Interpersonal	● ● ● ● ●
Presentation	● ● ● ● ○

EDUCATION

Art Center College of Design
Sep 2014 - present
INTERACTION / PRODUCT DESIGN

Relevant Coursework:
Brand Experience, Rapid Problem-Solving & Innovation

The University of Chicago
Sept 2011 - Apr 2014
ECONOMICS

Relevant Coursework:
Math Analysis, Linear Algebra, Economic Analysis, Sociology, Media Studies

The American School in London
June 2010 - June 2011
HIGH SCHOOL DIPLOMA

Relevant Coursework:
Economics, Statistics, Calculus, Physics, Chemistry, Architectural Design, Creative Writing

EXPERIENCE

Content Platform Startup   *Feb 2014 - present*
LOS ANGELES, CA
STRATEGY, MARKETING, UX + UI DESIGN

» Established branding and marketing strategy
» Executed UX design process from research to prototyping
» Developed opportunities to form key partnerships
» Created matching algorithm between users and content

Becker-Friedman Institute   *Jan 2014 - April 2014*
UNIVERSITY OF CHICAGO, IL
RESEARCH ASSISTANT

» Conducted experiments in experimental Economics
» Experimental design and data analysis

Rangel Neuroeconomics Lab   *Jan 2013 - Oct 2013*
CALIFORNIA INSTITUTE OF TECHNOLOGY, CA
RESEARCHER

» Conducted social and neurocognitive experiments
» Experimental design using advanced data simulation, sampling, and analysis techniques
» Presented seminar on cutting-edge neuroeconomics research

Intelligence for Humanity   *June 2012 - Sept 2012*
GENEVA, SWITZERLAND
CONSULTING, STRATEGY

» Supported collaborations to solve complex qualitative analytics problems in specialized groups
» Created/edited proposals, presentations, and data visualizations for international conferences

Mathema Analytics   *May 2011 - Sept 2011*
CHICAGO, IL
CRM, STRATEGY

» Managed customer/client correspondence and relations
» Developed strategy for capturing new clients
» Streamlined internal communications and information organization

Freelance/Independent Work   *May 2009 - Sept 2013*
LOS ANGELES, CA
GRAPHIC DESIGN, MARKETING

» Created small-business advertisements, sales material, and logos
» Freelance graphic art + design (received several design awards)

Our friend Mark used a lot of visual cues to make it easier for the reader to navigate and digest their résumé at a glance.

Jane Doe

Profile

Professional with international expertise in: customer service, pricing, and management. Dedicated to developing people and continuously improving business processes.

Experience

Leading company in the Energy Sector   2005 – Present

Dynamic and competitive international environment with strong foundation principles and values that constantly researches and innovates in the Energy Sector.

Leadership and People Development

- Lead the Organization for New Employees: accelerate the integration of millennial employees across business functions by providing professional development and networking opportunties.
- Reconceptualised the organisational design of the EPC as Team Lead, made it flatter and reduced headcount which simultaniously enabled people development.
- Developed business continuity processes in line with newly introduced global guidelines, ensuring preparedness for any potential disruption / disaster to fleet and fuel terminals beside service centers.
- Managed teams of 10+ to 40+ people across multiple locations. Identified people's strengths and weaknesses and provided meaningful growth opportunities.
- Led the Safety Committee of the department: revamped structure and content of safety communication. Introduced outside presenters to cross-functional audience, which resulted in people taking ownership.

Teaching and Coaching

- As Business Continuity Advisor for Customer Service for Europe, Africa and Middle East developed and conducted global training program with equivalents in 3 other zones to raise awareness around business continuity. This reduced risk of operational failure.
- Teacher of Economics in a Secondary School: developed course material and taught micro- and macroeconomics.

Mobile:
Email:

... Jane has been the best BVM [Business Project Manager] I have worked with to date [at the Energy Company]. Her attention to detail has resulted in successful, trouble-free implementations while maintaining a friendly and happy project team. ... [S]he is the model of how a BVM should operate.

Vendor working with the Energy Company

Can do attitude, high commitment, result oriented, people manager, great communicator. It has been a real pleasure to work with her over the last 3 years. Learnt a lot from Agi, and she has put a big signature to the pricing department for which she should be very proud of.

Supervisor during Team Lead position

Her drive, enthusiasm, willingness to listen, learn and change behaviours, her support for people, her loyalty and commitment to organizational goals [are her greatest strenghts].

Zone Manager while Accounts Receivables Manager

Jane Doe

Logistics Planning and Financial Management

- As Retail Accounts Receivables Manager for Europe, managed the collection of $500 M monthly for the retail business, minimising financial exposure.
- Analysed retail pricing for Europe and shaped micro and macro level strategy, enabling 0.5% market share growth in Germany and profitable change to new business model in Europe.
- Oversaw 24/7 fuel delivery planning operations (120+ trucks, 20+ terminal locations) as Delivery Planning Supervisor which ensured continued fuel supply to partners including service stations, bus, train and ferry companies.
- Organised business events for extensive audiences in country and abroad. Managed vendors, coordinated logistics & communication, and ensured compliance with stringent corporate framework.

Project Management

- As Business Project Manager in EPC, managed the replacement of the fuels pricing system for Europe which reached end of life and had to be replaced by a new application in the cloud. The project was a 4 country project, with incremental version upgrades (retrofit), impacting 4000 retail sites, lasting 18 months, costing $3 M. Delivered on-time, under-budget, and with no significant post-go-live issues.
- Introduced 'live' automated interface between the Energy Company and the German Market Transparency Unit, ensuring compliance with the legistlation issued by the Bundeskartellamt in 2013.
- Extended the automated fuel pricing capabilities for Germany, enabling elimination of shift work and focusing on strategy updates which contributed to gaining additional market share.

Education   2000 – 2005

- **Corvinus University – Master of Economics / Teacher of Economics:** Major: European Integration and World Economic Adjustment; Minor: Teacher of Business English.

SAMPLE P.A.V.E.S.
AND COVER LETTERS

Our friend Michael was in the military and then held a series of seemingly unrelated jobs throughout his career. He wasn't sure what this qualified him for so we took him through the PAVES exercise. Ultimately, he realized he was uniquely qualified to build sets for the theater. Here's his PAVES and, on the next page, how he translated it into a cover letter for a position he wanted.

Accomplishments

1. Being a father – Raising Lily has been an amazing journey and the experience has definitely transformed my perspective on the world and how I live my life.
2. Military service – Being in the military provided me a chance to see the world and get money for college, but self-discipline and self-worth is what I learned the most out of my time in the military.
3. Start up branch office for construction company – Setting up policy and procedures, departments and hiring employees and built a back log of $15million work of work within three years.

Experiences

1. Living abroad – Living in Germany for 3 years gave me the opportunity to experience and learn multiple European cultures and at the same time a better appreciation for my home and where I come from.
2. Musical theater – It gives me the freedom to be anyone I want to be with the excitement of performing on front of large groups of people, which in the business world helps build confidence in making presentations.
3. Learning to swim – When I was 14 I learned how to swim by jumping off 40 ft. cliffs, it had lasting effects on the way I lived my life as to not really conquering my fear but understanding it and learning how to channel it.

Interests

1. Sports – I love the competition and appreciate the unpredictability.
2. The arts – I enjoy going to shows, being involved with the theater, drawing, painting, singing & dancing, music, read
3. Healthy lifestyle – I eat good, exercise, play golf, kayak, run, cycle

Passion

1. Family - means everything to me I couldn't live with out them
2. Sports – I love the energy and competition that brings out the best
3. Art – The freedom to imagine and create what ever the mind wants
4. Life – The only constant is change and you never know what will happen next it can be scary but very exciting

Values

1. Honor
2. Respect
3. Courage

Skills

1. Good with my hands – I can rebuild engines, fix appliances, draw(although I am out of practice) and build a house
2. Sell – I have over 14 years of sales experience including negotiations and closing
3. Reading blueprints/directions – I have a strong attention to detail and am very thorough
4. Project management – managed multiple projects simultaneously with contracts ranging from $500.00 to over 2 million dollars. Setting budgets, ordering materials, scheduling crews, progress billings.

December 8, 20XX

La Jolla Playhouse
P.O. Box 12039
La Jolla, CA 92039

Attn: Human Resources Manager
Re: Deck Crew Position

I am writing to you because I believe my unique and diverse background would make me an ideal candidate for the deck crew position.

At my most recent position I was a division manager. I was responsible for securing contracts and managing the projects from start to finish. I maintained all related administrative paperwork, change orders, and progress billings. I coordinated with production staff, ensuring that projects were completed on time and under budget. These are all responsibilities that require a strong attention to detail and the ability to communicate clearly and concisely. I have:

- The ability to fix or build just about anything from both personal experience and work experience. I have re-built multiple cars from the ground up, designed and built multiple housing and light commercial projects, and I can even sew my own clothes.

- Experience reading blue prints, schematics, troubleshooting and repairing mechanical and electrical equipment.

- Military experience where I learned self-discipline and motivation. I am capable of being the leader or being lead, and understand the importance of being part of a team.

- Managed a sales staff of 5 and production crew of 30 men. I set goals and incentives for the team to increase sales and decrease costs to achieve optimum bottom line profits.

- Developed comprehensive budgets by analyzing construction documents to include but not limited to labor, material, and equipment.

I have an Associates of Arts degree and studied theater at Fullerton College and have always felt very passionate and interested in being involved with the arts. I love to draw and paint, make music and dance and as shakespeare once wrote "all the world is a stage and all the men and women are merely players" I want my next act to be with the La Jolla Playhouse.

I look forward to discuss in further detail my business experience in a personal interview.

Sincerely,

Michael Stewart

Our friend Peter took things a step further with regard to our advice to focus on benefits and literally created a checklist of what the company was looking for and put a check next to his capabilities. In his cover letter. If he really excelled in an area, he put a check plus. Talk about making it a no-brainer for someone reviewing résumés.

Why you should interview me

I am sure that you are receiving many applications, many from qualified professionals, explaining what they can bring to the team. Rather than telling you how creative, energetic, and innovative I can be, I've decided to share a few thoughts I have to demonstrate what I bring to the table.

Transition Effects

Consumers often want features that are at odds. For example, speed and battery life are important, but faster processors draw more power. What really matters is the *perception* of speed. Transition effects can create the illusion of responsiveness with low processing cost. I would like to conduct a study to clearly quantify this effect and incorporate the findings into future products.

Product Integration

There are many opportunities to integrate LG mobile phones with other product lines. What if LG televisions could subtly display Caller ID and SMS messages from your LG mobile phone? No more mad dashes to see if a call was important. How about an alert on your phone when your clothes are dry? Getting hot? Use your phone to crank up your LG air conditioner.

Point of Sale

Currently, at the point of sale, mobile phones on display tend to be non-functioning and organized by carrier. This makes product differentiation very difficult. I would like to identify key features that motivate customers and showcase those features in LG phones. While other phones lay dormant, customers can take pictures, watch videos, check their Facebook, and Tweet about the experience from the LG phones.

Overview

Experience

Product Dev. ✓
Product Planning ✓
Market Research ✓
Project Mgmt. ✓+
Product Mgmt. ✓+

Personality

Creative ✓
Energetic ✓
Innovative ✓
Passionate ✓
Collaborative ✓
Knowledgeable ✓
Leader ✓

Education

MBA ✓+

I feel that with its track record for innovation and exciting products, LG would be an amazing company to work for. I would like to know more about this position and hope you would like to know more about me beyond this letter and my attached resume.

Thank you,

ACTIVE WORDS FOR RÉSUMÉS.

Action words are an important ingredient for bringing your feature/benefit statements to life. What you do at work (or anywhere, actually) can be loosely grouped into 3 categories: 1) Creation; 2) Maintenance/preservation, and 3) Destruction.

1. CREATION	Added, advised, architected, authored, built, captured, commandeered, conducted, crafted, created, crystalized, cultivated, defined, designed, developed, devised, directed, doubled, drove, earned, engineered, established, expanded, expedited, forged, founded, generated, identified, imagined, improved, improvised, increased, initiated, innovated, installed, instigated, instituted, instructed, introduced, invented, launched, led, liaised, modernized, negotiated, organized, oversaw, promoted, provided, redesigned, revitalized, segmented, selected, sourced, started, structured, supervised, transformed, uncovered, widened, wrote, won.
2. MAINTENANCE/ PRESERVATION	Adapted, arranged, coached, commandeered, converted, coordinated, distributed, encouraged, enforced, ensured, executed, guided, implemented, improved, inspired, interpreted, managed, mediated, motivated, orchestrated, organized, promoted, revitalized, strengthened, structured, translated, widened.
3. DESTRUCTION	Cut, decreased, defeated, eliminated, eradicated, improved, liquidated, modernized, organized, phased out, redesigned, segmented, shortened, streamlined, transformed.

Then there are the bullsh*t action words which make you look like you are trying to hard to say something that might sound like BS. We put those in a category by themselves, and admit that they are sometimes necessary and even useful.

BS ACTION WORDS OR WORDS OF "EXECUTION"	Accomplished, achieved, attained, completed, consummated, delivered, demonstrated, exhibited, performed, received.	
UPCYCLED PHRASES	"Responsible for"	headed, in charge of, etc.
	"Duties include"	guide, head, oversee, steer, manage
	Example: guide peers in abc taskforce or initiative; head xyz project; manage 123 resources	
	"Involved in" or "involved with"	cooperate, engage, liaise between, mediate, mitigate, participate

Making a contribution, serving a larger purpose, sacrificing for x, excelling, participating in a cause (green, save the children, sustainable x, reduction/elimination of y), innovation, customer first, think differently, harmony, people development, locally-sourced, loyalty, diversity, inclusion, fair play, team spirit, flexibility

Increased sales/market share, developed new revenue streams/found new markets, decreased churn/turnover, zaccelerated growth, achieved more with same or fewer resources, made $, saved $, increased sales or profits, managed a budget well, *lowest total cost, lowest cost of ownership, ROI, ROA, profitability, up/cross-selling*

Introduced *strategic change management*, implemented vision, successfully managed the merger of x, changed aspects of corporate culture through _____ , balanced _____ excellence with meaningful growth opptys, contributed to the success of my virtual team by_____ , collaborated with peers to share knowledge, supported quality & execution, contributed to design, identified people's strengths & weaknesses, developed team through coaching & feedback, built confidence within team, influenced x, elected x of y club, managed # of employees, retained highest performers, actively looked for ways to mentor employees that were not direct reports, created a productive and satisfying team envt, managed x or y workgroups/projects, *trusted thought partner/advisor*

Increased social media followers from x to 10x, created or managed social media content, promoted X, created campaign for X, earned media, authored papers, secured/maintained global position, created IP, created or maintained a social media profile/ strategy/presence/blog, organized trade shows

REVENUE
+ / –

VALUES

BRAND +

THE
BENEFIT MILL
for Résumés

LEADERSHIP

EFFICIENCY +
WASTE –

CUSTOMERS

RISK –

Increased efficiency, reduced waste/downtime/operating costs, eliminated redundancy, improved processes, managed x better, innovated work flows, accomplished x for the first time, developed/created/designed/architected x, managed departments efficiently, made decisions with increased speed & less pain, created tools/methodologies, decreased gaps

Understood/anticipated/responsive to customer needs, built intimacy, tailored x, customized y, exceeded company expectations under difficult or unusual circumstances, solved difficult problems, translated client requests into logical design, led a diagnostic dialogue with clients leading to business and learning outcomes, *reliability, trust, intimacy, post-purchase satisfaction*

Reduced liability/exposure, established a safety record, removed headache, identified problems others didn't see, managed conflict, responded quickly to threats, capitalized on opportunities, trustworthy, dependable, low initial investment, *past experience reduces risk of future failure or derailing*

Buzz words in italics

NOW WHAT?

Readers of the first edition of our book told us, "I did it! I upgraded my résumé! It looks great! Now what?" We also heard, "Hooray! I have an offer. Now what?" The following tips are our way of answering both of those questions.

For those looking for a corporate gig...
If you feel you understand where you're headed and your résumé reflects that, here are some things you can do in addition to the recommendations in Chapter 2.

- *Identify the companies you want to work for based on:*
    - o *Size of the company (e.g. Fortune 1000 list; USAspending.gov, etc.)*
    - o *Industry publications and trade magazines (e.g. for tech companies look at Gartner Magic Quadrants, Forrester-Waves, IDC, etc.)*
    - o *Key words that match your abilities or desired position*
    - o *Company culture ("How to Tell if a Company's Culture is Right for You" is a great start. HBR, 21 November 2017.)*

- *Go to indeed.com and set up a search with notifications.*

- *Once you've identified potential corporate matches, uncover points of contact you have within those companies. LinkedIn is still the gold standard for doing this and it may be worth upgrading to their Premium service so you can expand your search network. Leverage your connections to make warm intros to people who are connected to your target company.*

- *Of course you should look at the company's website to find any open positions and, as already stated in Chapter 2, learn more about them. Sites like owler.com aggregate news about companies and are excellent resources for broadening your insights.*

- *Whether you find a posted job you want or not, call your target company. Reach out directly to the person heading the department in which you want to work. (e.g. If you are in finance, contact the CFO. If you are in HR, the VP of HR.)*

- *Why do this? Because many positions that show they are open are, in fact, already lined up for someone else. Many times, a company must post open positions, despite the reality that they already have someone in mind to fill the position. But a company may also have a new position available that they haven't written up yet. Calling to find out what's available may place you a step ahead.*

- *Yes, it can be a little scary to put yourself out there for possible rejection. That's why we suggest adopting an attitude of "Why Not?" And if you don't hear back, no worries. You took the bold step of putting yourself out there and that's going to make it easier the next time around. Your persistence will pay off.*

- *If you are working with a headhunter, do not rely solely on their efforts to land your next job. A headhunter's paying client is the company that needs a specific job filled. They may not be properly incentivized to find the perfect match for you.*

For those who already have a job offer:

Jobseekers have asked us "Should I negotiate the offer I receive?" Every book on negotiation and most people involved in hiring will say, "Yes, but..."

Here are the but's...

- *Negotiate within reason. Have these discussions with HR or recruiting, not the person for whom you'll be working. Companies generally make offers they believe are fair. If you are unhappy about something in particular, talking with HR or recruiting will keep the slate clean with your future boss.*

- *Ask where there is wiggle room. Companies are often willing to give you more for a bonus or an equity grant because that allows them to keep the salary level the same for your position and department, not upsetting similarly positioned employees. It also incentivizes you to work hard and stick around.*

- *Explain why you have an issue with the offer. "I currently have x and y at my current job, and I don't want to give these things up." Then just be quiet and wait for a response.*

- *Pick your fights. Try this approach: "There are two areas where this offer is lacking, and I'm willing to give on the one if you meet me on the other."*

Should you have a lawyer look over your offer?

Yes, to see if the contract left something important out. A good lawyer will point out omissions and where you could be at risk:

> *"There is no severance clause..."*
> *"This leaves you vulnerable here..."*
> *"In the event of a buyout, a merger, or bankruptcy you aren't guaranteed..."*

AND, whatever you do, do not tell the company you went to a lawyer. No one wants a litigious employee. As headhunter extraordinaire Andrew Ormand suggests, "Don't be an idiot. There is no benefit to creating tension for no good reason." Adopt the lawyer's concerns as your own when you go in to discuss the offer.

We hope that these additions save you time and help you focus in your job search. What other questions do you have for us? We'd love to hear those, as well as your jobseeking stories. You can find us and drop us a line on LinkedIn.

Who knows, your comments and questions just might make the 3rd edition.

THANK YOUS

We'd like to acknowledge that we built this book on the participation, ideation, feedback and good old trial and error of our friends/guinea pigs including Josh & Malia Kuss, Mitchell Zak, Carrie Phair, Joe Nagy, Jason Sigala, Michael Sigala, Agnes Fono, Peter Oneppo, the Human Aspirin, Golf Girl, Food Girl and huge swaths of the 2007 - 2014 Classes of UC San Diego's Rady School of Management. Thank you for being trusting and crazy enough to let us tinker with your careers. We also thank our illustrator and designer Chelsea Flaming who took our book from a giant Microsoft Word doc to reality. You not only put up with our endless revisions, you made our text entirely more readable. (we hope)

From Wendeline

Thank you to Alexander for all the input and suggestions. To Nikki for the patience and understanding that his mom was working on something important to her. Thank you to all the participants, students, and friends (you know who you are) that trusted me with résumés, life stories, and aspirations over many, many years at ISB, DukeCE, SSE, Thunderbird, Ericsson, DeLaval, and UCSD, among others. I reserve the biggest bit of gratitude to "The Universe" for putting Forrest into my life and allowing us to have this book as an excuse for connection and collaboration over almost a decade.

From Forrest

Wendeline, when I met you as my professor, I hit the lottery. Now, a decade later, I consider you a dear friend. Which means I've signed up for lifelong learning with margarita tabs subbing for student loans. I also have to thank my husband Rob, whose eye-rolling patience with my crazy ideas (like writing this book), and creative ability to make my ideas better, helps me grow every day. I'd also like to thank my parents for giving me a name attached to an expectation that one day I'd author a book. Consider that box checked. Mom, thank you for unleashing your English teacherness upon us and proofreading this book. And to my brother Steven, our original résumé guinea pig. Snakes + Cocktails + Podiums = Magic. Just as we mapped out, it's all coming together, man.

Printed in the USA
CPSIA information can be obtained
at www.ICGtesting.com
LVHW060913110923
757779LV00008BA/48

9 780999 637500